To Michael George

The Flying Piano Roll Man

Good Luck with Book 2 writing!

Hi Babbit
3-11-11

The Flying Piano Roll Man

Hi Babit

Copyright © 2010 by Hi Babit.

Library of Congress Control Number:		2010912080
ISBN:	Hardcover	978-1-4535-5897-3
	Softcover	978-1-4535-5896-6
	Ebook	978-1-4535-5898-0

All rights reserved. No part of this book may be reproduced or transmitted in any form or by any means, electronic or mechanical, including photocopying, recording, or by any information storage and retrieval system, without permission in writing from the copyright owner.

This book was printed in the United States of America.

To order additional copies of this book, contact:
Xlibris Corporation
1-888-795-4274
www.Xlibris.com
Orders@Xlibris.com

Contents

Chapter 1	The Years 1917-1931	7
Chapter 2	The Years 1931-1940	14
Chapter 3	The World War II Years: 1941-1945	33
Chapter 4	The Years 1946 to the Present Time	48
Chapter 5	The Piano-Roll Years	156
Chapter 6	The Flying Years	197
Chapter 7	My Inventions: Good, Bad, Indifferent, Questionable	236

Chapter 1

The Years 1917-1931

Today is the 18th day of August in the year 2009. In the Hebrew tradition, the number 18 is considered life. The Hebrew word for life is *chai*, and it happens that my Hebrew name is Chaim. For your understanding of how to say the word chai, you use a guttural sound, as if clearing your throat, to say that word. You do not use a *tch* sound to say chai. I'm sure you've heard that song from *Fiddler on the Roof*: "To life! To life! L'Chaim." So I'm about to start a story of my life from birth till the present time and my expectations for the future. I've been asked many times to write this story. I will attempt to do it now. I will try to remember things that happened in all these years, but I have to apologize if I forget some things. I guess my memory is selective!

I will be mentioning areas, street names, which may be unfamiliar to most readers; but for those who knew the areas and streets, they may enjoy reading about and reminiscing those times and places. It also helps to remind people that, although I'll be turning ninety-three years of age, that I can still remember most of the past. Should I say Thank God?

Before I start, I'd like to mention that I believe there is a saying about a person wearing multiple hats. I think that I may qualify in that category. I'd like to explain that I wear a lot of hats. I'm going to list the things I've done on one side of the page and place a title on the other side of the page.

Invented a device for aircraft and got a patent .... Inventor
Composed music .... Composer
Written songs .... Songwriter
Written lyrics for songs .... Lyricist
Made piano rolls since 1963 .... The Piano Roll Arranger
Done artwork (when I was young) .... Artist
Written articles .... Author
Had a photo business .... Photographer
Involved in court cases .... Detective
Had a leather-craft business .... Craftsman
Had a nailhead business for clothing .... Businessman
Learned flying—ratings-land-sea-glider commercial ...... Pilot
Tuning pianos every day .... Piano Tuner
Rehearse and play shows .... Musical Director
Played with bands, restaurants, etc .... Musician

All that I've listed above are things that you can also do if you have an interest like I have in learning and using your head to think problems out. Strive to learn and do something new. You never know when you're going to use that knowledge. My background is based on the desire to look for something new every day.

Back to my life story.

I was born in Brooklyn, New York, on November 9, 1917. Just as an aside, in a book called the *Billings Rollography*, volume 5 of the QRS history of pianists that made piano rolls for that company, it states that I was born in Brooklyn, New York, on November 9, 1897. Of course that makes me over one hundred years old. But I guess they call that a typo error.

I was born in the Brownsville section of Brooklyn, which was also known as the area where Murder Inc. originated. The building we lived in was on the northeast corner of Riverdale and Sackman streets. The only memory I have retained of the era is an incident (I guess you would call it a lynching) where a person was hung from the crossbar entrance to a lumberyard that was kitty-corner from our building. There was a big crowd there; that's all I can recall from that era.

Before I go any further in my story, I think I should tell you that my parents were Esther and Max Babich. And the rest of the family were me, the firstborn and the eldest of the siblings; Herman Bernard; then came Sylvia; then Reuben; and finally Rosalyn. Now when I mention them in the course of this tale, you will know who's who. Sylvia was born July 22, 1919. She was also born on Riverdale Avenue.

From there we moved to Chester Street, near Riverdale Avenue. My memory of the Chester Street apartment was that we bathed in the kitchen sinks and that there was a common toilet in the hallway. Reuben was born on April 3, 1923, at the Chester Street address.

From there we moved to Amboy and Newport avenues about 1924. It was there in 1925 that Rosalyn was born on May 1, 1925. I will refer to Rosalyn as Roz in the rest of the story. The landlord's daughter, Ida Gittelson, was my first piano teacher. Since we didn't have a piano, I practiced on her piano. I had three teachers in a couple of years. My second teacher was an Italian gentleman whose name I don't remember, but he gave me a tarantella to learn. I played it recently for some teachers, and they informed me that the tarantella is still being sold and used for teaching. I believe that teacher gave me lessons in our next location in East Flatbush.

My father, Max Babich, had a manufacturing company in New York City at 146 West Twenty-fifth Street between Sixth and Seventh avenues, where he made women's coats. Being financially successful, he bought a new two-family house in 1927 at 143 East Ninety-second Street in East Flatbush, and we moved there from Amboy Street. We lived on the second floor. The houses on that block were two adjoining, with an alley between them, with garages at the back end of the alley.

My parents bought a new O. W. Wuertz grand piano for the new house. That piano is now at my brother's apartment in the Palmaire area of Pompano Beach, Florida, with all the old music sheets and books. Rube is still an active sheet-music collector. He's also a stamp dealer. Although Rube is a sax player, with the availability of the old piano, he taught himself how to play the piano. I'm the piano tuner for that piano.

My third teacher was Frederick J. Bried, with a studio on Nostrand Avenue and Eastern Parkway in Brooklyn. While under his tutelage, I won a silver medal at Carnegie Hall in 1930. I have a certificate for that recital dated June 26, 1930. After I started playing with bands and I'd visit Mr. Bried, he would call me the jazz player. I was only with Mr. Bried for about a year or a year and a half, but he did give me some finger exercises to do that helped me get an ability that still serves me well. One exercise was stretching your fingers from thumb to pinky in front of the keys against the front rail. The second exercise was using your thumb and the pinky of one hand to stretch two fingers apart from the other hand, and bending the fingers back to crack the knuckles. Try it. It may help!

I have big hand stretches now so that instead of playing octaves—eight notes like most pianists do—my normal stretch is tenths, and this gives me sounds that most pianists can't get. I use that same kind of stretched chords in my musical arrangements. My daughter Laurie also studied with Mr. Bried, and we performed on a radio station some years later. The show was called *Live Like a Millionaire*, and I have a stub for that performance that reads forty-six dollars as our recompense for that day. What would that appearance pay today? I wonder.

In those days in East Flatbush, my first school was PS 189, where my only recollection was that I must have been a bad boy, because I recall hitting a teacher and being sent to the principal's office. Temper, temper! I don't remember the reason or the outcome. The next school was PS 219 on Clarkson Avenue. At that school I wanted to be in all the school plays and play the leading roles, because I had a bad case of stuttering, and I wanted to be able to correct it. Of course, because of that playacting, I had nicknames based on the roles I played. I was called Professor or Philosopher or whatever the role was. I don't think that the playacting helped my stuttering, but it got me some notoriety on the street block.

I rarely played on the street with the other kids, as I was usually down in the basement of our house building model airplanes and teaching myself photography. Maybe because of my stuttering and not wanting to be embarrassed, I just stayed in the basement and learned to construct things and learn other subjects. Years later, I learned how to cure the stuttering. That's a later story.

After PS 219, I went to Winthrop Junior High, where I played piano in the auditorium. Sylvia, who also played piano, would sometimes play duets with me. I was also the school artist and did most of the artwork on the classroom blackboards. I liked to draw. Still do! I think that the reason I went to Erasmus Hall High School was to major in art. I had heard it was the best school to go to for artwork. I don't think I ever majored in art, but I did a lot of drawing, including three-dimensional artwork for my inventions and devices.

In the fall of 1930, I went to the Erasmus Hall High School Annex, on Lenox Road and East Fortieth Street. One day in the gymnasium I was playing the piano, and a fellow student came to me and asked me if I would like to join his band. It was a novel idea, and I said OK. I guess that was the beginning of my musical career.

That student was Max Rubin, and he lived in Borough Park on Forty-ninth Street between Ninth and Tenth avenues. The band had Mac on drums, me on piano, Irving Feitelowitz on saxophone, and Al Rosenberg on trumpet. It was a nice little band. My family owned a 1928 Oldsmobile then, a stick shift car. My mother, being more outgoing than other mothers of that day, took up driving and drove all of us anywhere we had to go. She drove me to Mac's house when we had rehearsals there.

1930 was another memorable year, because that meant that I was turning thirteen years old on November 9. What do you do for your thirteenth birthday? Of course, being Jewish, your parents make a bar mitzvah party for you for the honor of becoming a man. My parents prepared a big bar mitzvah celebration at the Deluxe Palace on Howard Avenue, near Eastern Parkway in Brooklyn. I have that family portrait. We held a lot of family celebrations at that catering hall.

Chapter 2

The Years 1931-1940

*I*n the early 1930s my daily routine was to go to high school in the morning, then go to New York City in the afternoon to my father's factory to learn a new trade of cloth cutting and pattern making. After work I went home for dinner, and then changed my clothes and went to Borough Park where our band would play for dances. If I remember, we only got about a dollar or two for the night. The question now is, would kids today do what we kids did then?

Working in my father's factory, I became a clothing cutter and pattern maker. The clothing cutter that my father employed taught me how to use the two types of machines in use then. You had a round-blade and a straight-blade machine. That depended on what type of material you were cutting. If you were going to cut rayon linings, which were about two inches high, then you used the round blade machine. If you were going to cut the thicker woolen material for the outside coats, which piled high to about four to six inches, then you used the straight up and down machine.

Then I was taught how to make patterns and how to design clothing. Another thing that I learned was mathematics. I didn't do well in algebra in school, but working with figuring out about yardages in the garment line, I became more adapted to math, and I do believe it helped me in making the piano rolls, because of having to figure out punches to fit the beats of my arrangements.

One of the sewing-machine operators in my father's shop was an owner of a hotel up in Lake Huntington in Sullivan County, New York. That area, of course, had all kinds of names, such as the Catskills, the Borsht Belt, the Jewish Alps, or just the Mountains, and was known as the place where most of the great comics got their start. A lot of the big bands got their start there too. It was a great breeding and learning area, and there are lots to tell tales about.

That's where we got our first summer job for the band—at the Crestwood Hotel in Lake Huntington in the summer of 1931. We were paid three dollars a week, room and board. You may laugh at the amount of pay we received, but let's face it, it was 1931, when you could buy ten gallons of gas for a dollar for your automobile, or go to the movies or on the subway for a nickel. That was the start of our careers with music. All I can say is, I went away every summer and got my summer's vacations paid for. That, of course, lasted until the draft started just before World War II.

The summer of 1940 was spent at the Kenmore Lake Hotel in Livingston Manor, and the following summer of 1941, I was in the Army at Fort McClellan, Alabama.

If I remember correctly, the Labor Day weekend of 1940 brought the news of Germany invading Poland. I began thinking of defense jobs. But more later.

That first summer's job at the Crestwood was a very interesting experience. A lot of times, after we finished playing in the ballroom, or what was called the casino (which had nothing to do with gambling, but it was where we would play dance music and put on shows), we would go visit other hotels and watch other bands. I was envious watching other piano players play for singers and playing without music and thinking that I would like to do that too.

Today, it's another story! Now I've gotten into the habit of playing for shows without written music, because after all the rehearsals, I know the music score. I have to mention another reason for not reading music; and that is, if an entertainer goofs, I just follow them or cover them. I've seen shows where the entertainers goof and watched pianists scrambling with the music. I have to say that when an entertainer goofs, they quickly look at the piano player like it's the pianist's fault. I just had to explain! Before a show goes on I tell the entertainer that if they goof, just keep on going and I will follow them. I usually get thanks. I'd like to explain about goofs. If the entertainer skips a line or section, or changes the pitch of singing, it would be apparent if he or she stops and looks at the pianist, which happens at times. That's why I tell the entertainer that if he or she goof, just keep on going and I will cover them with the changes.

One nice day we went out in a small rowboat to the middle of Lake Huntington. While fooling around I accidentally fell into the water. When the boys yelled to me that I was swimming the wrong way, I started to flounder and sink. Mac was a junior lifeguard, and both he and Al jumped into the water to save me from drowning. I was not a great swimmer. Mac was pulling me up, and Al was pulling me down, and I was drinking a lot of water. They finally got me into the boat and back to the shore. I never forgot that close call. I count my blessings!

Whenever my folks would come up to visit, I would tell my mother to tell people I was sixteen years old so I could get dates with girls. Ha-ha! My two cousins, Jack and Hymie Babich, came up on their motorcycles to visit me. I guess that's when I took a liking to motorcycles. Airplanes and motorcycles were for me. In later years I did own motorcycles, and then an airplane. I guess I liked speed and excitement! I didn't like to sit still and was always on the go. There is a slang expression of having ants in your pants. I could throw in a Jewish word *shpeelkess*, which means the same as "ants in your pants." It's for someone who doesn't sit still and is always on the go.

In the early 1930s I used to go out to the Floyd Bennett Field in Brooklyn on Flatbush Avenue and go up for a three-dollar-sightseeing flight. Roz reminds me that I took her there for a flight too. I think that I also took Syl for a flight. Those flights were usually over Coney Island, which was the well-known tourist attraction. Those years were depression times, but I always seemed to find some money for those trips. Well, I'm still a flight nut and follower to the point that when my ear picks up the sound of an aircraft motor, I unconsciously look up to see where the plane is. I heard that's an instinctive movement of most pilots.

The same thing happens with motorcycle sounds. I guess the word "habit" applies to things we like to do. We react to our favorite sounds. "The sound of music" always gets my attention; whether I'm in the movies or restaurants, I always listen for musical arrangements.

I did own about three motorcycles, but after the second accident, I decided to give it up. I wasn't looking for a third accident to happen. Instead of riding motorcycles, I decided a few years later to take up flying and had a lot of experiences that were enjoyable and fruitful, and sometimes scary and frightful.

More about my flying a bit later.

My first attempt at inventions came about from making model airplanes. Anyone who knows airplanes knows that the ailerons at the end of the wings make a wing bank for turns. So I figured that if you put two ailerons in the middle of the wing and made them work together up or down, a fighter plane could then make a quicker move to avoid an enemy plane. Of course, we only made World War I airplane models then. I started making those models about the time I started my first year of high school.

I brought that idea to the aero club in high school, and the teacher said that it would never work. I didn't really know anything about aerodynamics. But about a year later, I saw a photo in the *New York Times* of the new DC-3 with the new air brakes. Today we call them flaps. What can I tell you, I'm always ten years ahead of the times.

I have to mention that building model airplanes or doing photography or doing leather-craft work, such as lacing wallets or photo frames, was something that I always went after. I always liked to learn new things;

and to this day, even though I'm in my nineties, I still go after something new. But you had to have one little thing, and that is called patience! You just can't rush learning. Someone once mentioned to me that "patience is a virtue, but too much of it can hurt you." They were right. But it seemed a bit strange that although I had the patience to do these things, I would sometimes try to rush the learning, and I'd end up defeating my learning process. But that's life. I guess.

Because of the way I made piano rolls, it was very necessary to have patience. You held notes down while the machine punched slowly, very slowly, the amount of punches to make each beat. There was no way to speed up making a piano roll. It was a slow, tedious, and boring process, but I could make a piano do what a human being could not do. I will explain more fully in the chapter on piano rolls.

I used to tell my music students that even though the selection called for rapid playing, they had to start slow and let the fingers get accustomed to the movement of that notation passage; you have to go slow first before you go fast. That applied to my flying instruction as well. Certain maneuvers had to be done slowly so that you could get the feel of it. If you tried to do it quickly in an airplane, it could lead to dire results. You've got to go slow before you can go fast. You have to repeat that phrase to students, in music or flying, over and over. Maybe that also applies to learning how to drive a car. A baby crawls before it walks. That applies to learning.

Sometimes I don't follow my own advice. I learned how to drive an automobile in five minutes. How? I always watched my father or mother drive. In those days we had a stick shift car. Well, one day my father parked the car between the two houses and blocked the alley. Someone called and asked us to please move the car. I volunteered, saying that I knew how to move the car. I went down, got into the car, started the motor, then stepped on the clutch, and put the car in gear. I stepped on the gas, and the car didn't move. I raced the engine, and the car still didn't move, so I took my foot off the clutch, and the car jumped forward. Now I had my lesson. I stepped on the clutch, shifted into reverse, and slowly released the clutch. I moved the car back, and then I tried it forward, and now I knew how to drive. Boy, am I smart! Ha-ha!

After I graduated high school, I went to work in a Chinese restaurant in Jamaica, Queens, New York, on Jamaica Avenue, a very busy street under the elevated trains. Those elevated trains are now gone. I was with a six-, seven-, or eight-piece band. We played for lunch and then took a break of a few hours, then played dinner, and later a show. I don't remember how many days of the week we worked, but I do remember that our pay was about eighteen or twenty dollars a week. In between lunch and dinner, I usually went to the movies for about a nickel or dime—I don't really recall. I did not have a car those days, so it was a lot of subway riding; we played there about a year.

I joined the music union, local 802, in 1935; and I used to go to the union floor, which was, I think, first in some building on Broadway, and then moved to the Roseland Ballroom on West Fifty-second Street, between Seventh and Eighth avenues in Manhattan. I played what they called club dates, such as bar mitzvahs, weddings, dances, etc. and it was usually just weekend jobs.

I used to go up and down Broadway calling on agents, looking for more work. I finally latched on to a job as rehearsal pianist for an upcoming Broadway show called *Caribbean Cruise*. I believe the year was either 1937 or 1938. Since George Gershwin had come out with his *Porgy and Bess* show in 1935, and it was an all-black show, another composer, Donald Heywood, tried to come out with an integrated show, which I think was the first of its kind.

The male lead was screen actor Sonny Tufts. I don't remember who the leading lady was. I rehearsed the Nicholas Brothers every day. You may not remember the name of that dance team, but it was a pleasure to rehearse them. I was enthralled in the way they danced. They were famous for making jumps and splits. You may see them in some old musicals of the late 1930s and 1940s. I believe that Lena Horne was also in the show, and I probably rehearsed her too. If a new song was needed, Donald Heywood would sit down at the piano, write something out, and give it to me to play for the cast. We did a lot of auditions, but I don't think that show ever opened. Anyway it was a great experience.

Looking at some old photographs, I came across one that showed I was in a five-piece band. We were playing in a restaurant up on Dyckman Street in Upper Manhattan. From my appearance I am thinking that it would be about the year 1936. Somehow I recall the name of the drummer as George Rosales. Why, I don't know. The trombone player was named Bunny something. I don't recall his last name, but I do remember buying an old 1928 Studebaker with him as partners. The car had the spare tires (two of them) in the front fender wells and had circular steel braces to hold the tires on its hubs. One day while driving, I had a flat tire and noticed the steel rim rolling down ahead of the car like a hoop wheel. That's all that I remember from that picture. This job could have been before that Chinese-restaurant gig in Jamaica, Queens.

My summer jobs in the Catskills started with the Crestwood Hotel in Lake Huntington in 1931. Then we played at the Moonglow Inn in Loch Sheldrake in 1932. In 1933, we played at Anderson's Hotel in Monticello. That hotel was on the road to Kutsher's Country Club, where I played many years later. In 1934, I think we had a job in a hotel in Fallsburgh, where we played only half a summer; and then for some reason, we changed hotels. I don't remember those hotel names. In 1935, I believe we played in a hotel called the Grand in Hurleyville. I think it was across the road from that well-known place called Brown's Hotel where Jerry Lewis made his start.

I have to say that while playing in those different hotels, I didn't play with the original members of the '31, '32 or '33 band. I don't remember the names of all the other orchestras that I played with on those jobs. We were hired to do a summer job, and we went. I think you could call them pickup bands. Agents or band leaders would try to put together bands, and that was a way that we met and got friendly with a lot of musicians. I have to say again that I went away every summer and got my vacation paid for. That is one advantage of learning music!

In 1936, I played at Gluck's Hillside Inn in Kiamesha Lake. That was a nice place and considered one of the more affluent hotels. The bands in those days were given rooms at the back of the casinos. They were not the greatest of rooms, with bare open studded walls. They were not like guest rooms. After World War II when the Concord Hotel opened, the Gluck's Hillside Inn became the helps' quarters for the Concord Hotel personnel.

In 1937 I played at some hotel in Glenwild; that was on the road between the old Route 17 and Woodridge. I have to interject here about a gimmick most bands had in those years. We would put on a benefit show to get some extra money. Well, at that hotel we put on a benefit; and since those benefits included getting some entertainers from other hotels, we had a young drummer, Buddy Rich, sitting in. In 1938 I played at Klein's Hillside in Parksville. I played there again in the years 1967 and 1968. The leader then was Sy Sugar.

I did play one winter's session at the Flagler Hotel in South Fallsburgh. In those years, the Flagler was considered one of the better or more prestigious hotels of the day. It may have been 1936. We had an entertainer who was both a comic and a singer, and he did a selection called "Khaki Moon." It had a double-entendre meaning. It was supposed to be in Hawaii; but in Jewish metaphor, it means "look at him, the big shot," or some similar connotation. The comic/singer's name was Billy Hodes. People think I'm a whiz at remembering names; but the truth is, I have to ask some old-timers, or rely on looking up items.

For instance, I couldn't remember Billy Hodes's name at the Flagler. I was rehearsing a show recently, and one of the scenes coming up at that show was to take place in a kitchen. My habit was throwing in musical jokes, as I call them, to fit the scene; and I started to play an old Jewish song called "Essen, mir gehen essen," which when translated means "Eating, we're going to eat." That song was associated with the Borsht Belt hotels. One of the cast mentioned that he used to play with someone named Billy Hodes at the Flagler. I stopped and thanked him and explained that I was trying to remember the name of the singer and comic that I played with in 1936 or 1937. That entertainer told me that he worked with Billy Hodes during the years 1947 and 1948.

I had a close call experience that winter at the Flagler. I always did a lot of hiking when I was up at those hotels. One day I decided to hike along the old O&W railroad tracks from Fallsburgh to Woodridge. At one point along that route was a tunnel that the trains ran through. I asked some workers who were outside of that tunnel if there were any trains due to go through that day, and they said no, that in the winter there were very few trains. It was a single-track tunnel, and I started to walk through there. I figured it was quicker and easier than going over the mountain. I was almost to the end of the tunnel when I heard a train coming toward me at a fast speed. I just made it to the outside as the train roared by! It was just an engine and tender. There was no room for clinging to the wall. So again, I was lucky. I'll count my blessings!

In 1939 and 1940, I played at the Kenmore Lake Hotel in Livingston Manor. The leader was Red Rosen. My roommate for those two years was Red Buttons. The entertainers besides Red Buttons were Bobby and Irma Fay (whose brother was Herbie Fay of old TV fame) and a female singer.

In those days before World War II, all hotels had a staff of entertainers who stayed there the whole summer. We had to put on shows or games almost every night. That changed after the war, and it then became one-nighters for entertainers. The Broadway agents had a field day, because they booked entertainers for a single date or a double date for a night. Now forty or fifty years later, entertainers are still doing one-nighters or doing a double for the night. Tradition!

The mode of transportation in those days were either you drove up to the mountains in a car, or you used a hackie (private cars where you paid the driver), or you came by train or bus. The train was the infamous O&W (Ontario and Western) line that you got at Weehawken, New Jersey. I used that line many times in traveling to and from the hotels. It usually was a long day's trip. Take the subway to Manhattan, go to the ferry on the Hudson, take the ferry to Weehawken, New Jersey, and then take the train. To some it was a scenic ride, and to some it was a necessity.

I forget what kind of schedules there were, but I think it was mostly a one-time arrival about late afternoon, and almost all the stations in that resort area had cars from the hotels awaiting the arrival of the trains to take visitors to their reserved hotels. Some may say that the drivers were also what we call "hawkers," to try to induce people to go to their respective hotels. Friday evenings were usually the busiest times there because of the weekend visitors and visiting husbands! Sometimes the Friday-evening arrivals were called "the hard-on special." That's known as Borscht Belt humor.

When you drove and took the old Route 17, which you picked up in New Jersey after taking Route 4 from the George Washington Bridge, you passed Suffern, New York, then usually made a stop at the Red Apple Rest. That was a meeting place for most people. There was another place called Miller's 666 also on Route 17, but another fifteen or twenty miles north, and it was another substitute choice of meeting. There was a well-known police speed trap on Route 17 near a small town that was called—I think—Old Bush or Pine Bush. Then there was the famous Wurtsboro Hill, which was known for getting a lot of overheated cars stuck on that road. Finally came Monticello, which had turn-offs on Route 42 north for the Fallsburgh hotels; or Route 42 south for the Swan Lake hotels; or continue on Route 17 to the areas north of Monticello for the Liberty, Parksville, and Livingston Manor and Roscoe hotels. Today, it's only a memory, with maybe one or two places trying to stay alive. Of course, there's still the Monticello racetrack, which I believe is now a casino and gambling place. There's talk of rejuvenating the area with casinos, but I'm afraid that politics will either kill it or cure it.

In 1937 I bought my first motorcycle. It was a '45 Harley-Davidson. I better explain that it was called a '45, because it had a forty-five-cubic-inch engine. I rode it quite a bit. On a trip back from Lakewood, New Jersey, one time, I forgot to put the necessary oil in the engine; and it froze up on me. I called my cousin Jack Babich and told him what happened, and he came and towed me back in to Brooklyn.

I brought my bike to Carl's Motorcycle Shop on Linden Boulevard in Brooklyn where I learned how to take it apart and fix it. But I don't recall keeping it. I did buy another motorcycle in 1938. That was a real gem. It was, I was told, the last model made of that kind. It was a 1935 single-cylinder 30.50-cubic-inch engine Harley-Davidson with short handlebars and a top speed of only fifty-five miles per hour. That motorcycle saved my life. But that's a later story.

When I was at the Kenmore Lake Hotel, I had that motorcycle, and I used to practice running around the baseball field, making short stops and quick turns in anticipation of any road mishaps. But it didn't help when I really had a head on collision in 1941 when I was in the army. That's also a later story. I didn't spend much time at the hotel taking advantage of the facilities, because I was usually traveling around the countryside looking for new scenic spots and taking photos. I guess I had the same habit of not staying at the hotel as I had with not staying at home or playing on the street where I lived in Brooklyn.

That Harley was an easy bike to ride. I remember once when I went with a motorcycle club from Brooklyn to Staten Island, and I rode around the sloping walls of an empty reservoir. I have a photo of that incident. At Coney Island I used to see some motorcycle exhibitions of cyclists riding around the inside of a ball, and I guess I wanted to try the same thing. The difference was that the reservoir's sides were slanted at forty-five degrees where the Coney Island ball riders made inside loops. I didn't try that type of riding.

In 1937, I played at Ritter's Hotel in Lakewood, New Jersey, for the winter season, which coincidentally was where I had a few months earlier my first motorcycle incident. Lakewood, New Jersey, was a big resort area for New Yorkers and for people from Pennsylvania, too. There were a lot of hotels on Madison Avenue, with a lot of entertainers, and it was a very busy area. The entertainers were the same ones who did the summer hotels in the Catskills or the Mountains.

I remember going out with bands to some places in Connecticut to play at some roadhouses, but I don't really remember the years. I only tried being on the road a few times, and I didn't like it. I had a few calls from some of the big bands to travel with them, but I had too much work in the New York area, and it didn't pay for me to travel. After seeing movies and reading stories of how the big bands lived and traveled on the road, I was glad that I stayed home and worked locally.

Every summer I would meet a girl, and then see her back in the city. But most times nothing came of it since I was always busy working. If I remember correctly, most of the girls I met lived in Manhattan or Queens or the Bronx, but never in Brooklyn.

In 1938, I was strolling through the park (Prospect Park in Brooklyn) one fine day, and I met my future wife. I liked walking through the park, and I happened to pass a girl sitting on a bench and it looked like she was crying. I hesitated and then went over to her and asked if there was something wrong, and could I help? We got to talking and walking around the park, and then I walked her home to 299 Lefferts Avenue. I then went home to East Ninety-Second Street.

In those days, I did a lot of walking. I used to walk to Erasmus Hall High School from East Ninety-Second Street to Church Avenue and Flatbush Avenue. It had to be at least three to four miles or more. I also used to walk to my cousin's store on Stone Avenue in Brownsville, which was also two to three miles.

Speaking of my cousin, his name was Al Sinrod; and when we were kids, we would take the subway and go visit all the museums in Manhattan and the Bronx. It was only a nickel in those days, and it was very safe for kids to travel. I also used to rent bicycles and ride around Brooklyn. I had plenty of leg exercises biking or walking.

My cousin Al and I composed a song sometime in the late '30s. My first song was called "The Moon above Us." We had a verse and chorus. In the old days, a lot of songs had a verse and chorus. Sometimes the verse was nicer than the chorus. Although the words of that song might be considered corny today, some of the words of today's songs are more ridiculous. It's a waltz, and I play it occasionally.

I was the only one in the family who never stayed home. I was always going someplace. My sisters and brother knew everyone on the block. They played in the street with their friends or visited each other's home or listened to the radio and knew all the songs. Me, I was out traveling someplace else. Like I said before, when I played the hotels for the summer jobs, I spent my spare time traveling around Upstate New York or Pennsylvania instead of taking advantage of the activities and facilities of the hotels and mixing with the guests. If I did meet a girl that I wanted to be friendly with, then I might stay at the hotel and not travel.

The later years of the '30s when I met Florence Schneider at Prospect Park and started dating her, I began to change my habits. There was many a time that Florrie and I would go to Prospect Park to hear the famous Goldman Band. Goldman wrote a march called "On the Mall," which people would whistle and sing the only words, which were "la-la-la." I did use that march in a show here where I live, a few years ago. That band played all the boroughs of New York, and it was a good evening's outing. I was lucky that Florrie liked the same type of music that I did, mostly classical and good Broadway music. Those were the days when you could go to parks and enjoy the available activities.

In 1938 when I bought my nice Harley and was going places with it, I took Florrie with me on some of my travels, and we went to Upstate New York, New Jersey, and other places. I took plenty of photos in those days, because I did my own developing and printing. I still have thousands of negatives of the '30s, '40s, etc. There was an abandoned place they called Dick's Castle, which was a nice place to visit since it over looked the Hudson River. It was somewhere on the east side of the Hudson near Poughkepsie, New York. I wonder if it's still there. It was fun traveling both sides of the Hudson River with its picturesque scenery.

With the news of the European shenanigans going on, I started planning what to do in case there was trouble. I went to the Haller School of Welding, on Bergen Street in Brooklyn to learn how to weld in case I could get a defense job. I also went to a school in Long Island City in Queens for diesel engineering. I want to add that I also went to a Brooklyn high school for aircraft engineering and learned to use machinery, which came in handy later on when I used a friend's machine shop to build the prototypes for my airplane parking device invention.

In late fall of 1940, about October or November, I took my motorcycle and drove up to Brockton, Massachusetts. It was already getting cold up there, and I wore leather riding pants, and remembered using newspaper pages inside my riding jacket for warmth, like my cousin Jack Babich had told me. Because of the cold weather I would sometimes ride while sitting on my hands and making turns by shifting my body. I was lucky that I had a good balanced motorcycle. Reflecting back on doing that kind of riding, I think it was kind of stupid.

I got a job as a clothing cutter on poplin material, making jackets. I designed a reversible jacket for Florrie, with a fur-edged hooded-and-zippered jacket. (I have to say again that I was about ten years ahead of my time.) I don't know where that jacket is today, but I think that my daughter has it somewhere in her closet. I stayed at my cousin's house in Brockton for about three or four months.

Speaking of Brockton, I should mention that I had relatives in Taunton, Massachusetts, which was only about fifteen miles south of Brockton. They had a big farm there (the kids, who I believe are the grandchildren, still own the place), and I remember spending a few summers and winters there. Those visits were back in 1928 and 1929. They had an outdoor privy, and it sure was cold going out there in the winter nights in my long johns. I learned to farm and even got up early to go with my uncle at 4:00 a.m. to the food market in Brockton in his Model T Ford truck to sell the produce from his farm.

I had a girl friend in Taunton, with whom I used to correspond, and I wish I could remember her name, but memory diminishes. I remember seeing the new movie *Flying Down to Rio* and began playing those great tunes. "The Carioca" was a great piano piece, which I used to show off fast technique. I should have made a piano roll of that piece. The tango "Orchids in the Moonlight" is a great number to play. Also the title song "Flying Down to Rio" would have made a great piano roll.

 Years later, about 1949, I took my daughter and her cousin Judy for a trip around the New England area. We went to Cape Cod, Plymouth, and then to Brockton and Taunton. I showed them where I used to work, both in Brockton and the farm in Taunton where I learned how to farm when I was a young kid

Chapter 3

The World War II Years: 1941-1945

The early part of January 1941 is hazy and vague. I was working, seeing Florrie, and traveling around. Then came more news about the war in Europe and about the draft starting, and I again began looking for defense work—just in case. However, they did start the draft, and that's when I won the lucky number—I was called in the first draft.

Florrie and I decided to get married, and we did on January 28, 1941. It was a small wedding and we had a small reception at her brother Willie's house on Church Avenue in Brooklyn. We had our little honeymoon at a Brooklyn hotel. I was supposed to be in the army for only a year. We thought it wasn't a big deal. We figured on her coming down to live with me near the camp.

I had to report to the selective office on January 30, 1941, for induction. I had to go to Lexington Avenue in Manhattan for that. Going through all the tests, I finally got to the psychiatrist's section, where I was asked if I had any mental disorders. First I said no. Then I asked the person if stuttering was a mental disorder. He asked me if I stuttered. I knew what was going to happen. I answered, "M-m-m-m-m-most of the-the-the time." He put a big "R" on my induction paper, and I thought I was going home. Ha-ha-ha! An hour later, they called me and said that I was in the army. Shucks! I called Florrie and told her what happened. I told her that I was going to be sent to Camp Upton out on Long Island.

Florrie came with me to the train terminal at Flatbush and Atlantic avenues in Brooklyn to see me off. It was winter, and we were sent out to Camp Upton in Yaphank, Long Island, and put in tents. I think we were there for a week; my family and wife came out to visit me at the camp. But a week later, we were put on a train and shipped down to Fort McClellan, Alabama.

I was now with the Twenty-seventh Division, and in Company I of the 106th Infantry. About a week later, we got out in the company street for duty, and the CO asked if there were any musicians in the outfit. Of course, I raised my hand and said that I'm a musician. I was sent to the band section and thought they would give me a drum to play, since I'm a piano player. Instead they gave me a glockenspiel! In case you don't know what a glockenspiel is, it's like a U-shaped small xylophone with steel bars that you hit with a roundball mallet. I think another name for it is "lyre." You wear a truss, like for a flag, but that's where you put the long bar of the glockenspiel.

Now, I'm in the 106th Infantry band, and I'm happy. We don't go out in the field for exercises. All we do is get up in the morning for reveille, then go back to the tent, go for breakfast, then play the troops out, go back to the tent, and wait for noon. Then we play the troops back in for lunch, then play the troops out. At 4:00 p.m. we play the troops back in, then supper, and then we play retreat, and we're finished for the day. That's what the routine was every day. What an easy life! We never did any army field training and stayed mostly around our tents. We did do some playing for the officer's club.

In March or April, I rented an apartment in Anniston, Alabama, the nearby town, and sent for Florrie to come and live with me there. She came, and we met a lot of people there. We belonged to the JWB, the Jewish Welfare Board. I also got to play on the local radio station WHMA. I had a weekly half-hour program of just piano music. Weekends were spent with the JWB outings, or meeting with friends. We got friendly with the Wetzels, who were from Buffalo, New York. That was Eileen and Richard Wetzel. We all lived in the same building, which I think was on Quintard Street or Avenue. It's a funny name, but I think my memory is right. In May my father, mother, and sister Roz drove down from New York to visit me at camp; and my sister reminds me that she was scared on the trip, because they took the newly built Blue Ridge Mountain roads, which had no guardrails.

There was an eatery we went to in Anniston called the Dugout. When I was off base, we would usually meet our friends there and listen to the jukebox. Florrie's favorite numbers were "Let Me Call You Sweetheart," "Darling, You and I," and "Stars Fell on Alabama." The Dugout was our favorite meeting place besides the JWB outings and such.

I used to hear someone use the phrase "it makes no never mind," which I assumed meant "I don't care" or some such meaning. I always remembered that phrase, and I'm assuming that it's a southern-area phrase. In later years, I decided to write a song using that phrase. That's another song that I didn't do anything with, but maybe I will start trying to do something with it soon. I tried to get a country or hillbilly effect type of song.

In May or June, the Twenty-seventh Division was sent on what they called the Louisiana Maneuvers for training purposes in the field. Our band was selected to stay behind and do guard duty. They gave us .45 guns with no clip in them; and when we asked what we would have to do in case of any emergency, they said, throw rocks! What an army! One night while on guard duty I fell asleep and was punished by having to do KP.

In June, I asked my mother to ship my motorcycle down from New York. Meanwhile Florrie had to go back to New York. Why, I don't recall. I believe that was the time I wrote another song, "Away from You," about being away from her and the hometown of New York. Anyway in July of 1941, I got a furlough and drove to New York on my motorcycle. I took photos going up and coming back. About two weeks later, after I came back from furlough, I went with the local motorcycle club to Atlanta, Georgia, to see the races. It was August 3, 1941.

On the way home, it became dark, and it had just rained. The night was pitch-black, and the headlight on that cycle was not the greatest. It was about 9:00 p.m. Following me were two guys on a motorcycle with a sidecar. We were getting close to Anniston when I came down a hill and started up the next hill. I saw a spare tire that was mounted on the back of a car in front of me, and the last thing I remember thinking was, "It's rubber, and I'll bounce." Boy did I bounce! I hit the car and went through its back window, but then fell down alongside the motorcycle. I was lucky that I wasn't impaled in that window. I found out later that I hit an old 1931 Chevy that had broken down and was stuck on the road. I took some photos a few months after that of my motorcycle and saw that the front wheel was even with the headlight. I would guess my speed was about forty-five to fifty miles per hour when I hit. That accident saved my life. I will explain more later.

I was out for a minute or two, and when I came to, lying there, I could see that the light of the cycle was still on, and the motor was still running. I was told later by the other two riders that they heard the crash but didn't see me until almost being on top of me. They shut the engine and the light. Also coming up was a bus, which almost ran into us. On board was a medical officer from the camp hospital. I was lucky. He came to assist me. He asked if I could walk. I tried, first with the left leg, and then when I tried to walk on my right leg, I realized that it was broken.

I was also lucky that I have fat legs and was wearing my storm laced boots over my tight britches. Because of how I was dressed, I had only simple complete fractures of the tibia and fibula bones in my right leg. To reconstruct the accident, I had the habit of riding the right brake with the heel of my right boot; when I hit the car and was catapulted up into its rear window, my right leg got caught in the crash bars of the motorcycle and prevented me from going through and being impaled in that back window. My britches and boots acted like a cast. I had head cuts and chin cuts. They called for an ambulance from camp and took me to the station hospital there. Now I was a patient in the hospital. My chin was ripped open, and my scalp was also cut open, and I had a small cut under my left eye. I wonder about that cut because in those days, I had a cloth helmet on and wore goggles. I looked more like an airplane pilot than a cyclist. The lens of the right goggle broke, but I had the cut under the left eye?

I had a cast that stretched from my toes to my hip. One day the doctor came in, made a slit in the lower part of the cast, and put some tongue depressors in. When the older doctors came through the ward every day, I heard the young doctor who treated me telling the others, "This is the boy with the angulation." I didn't know what he meant, but I found out later when I had a chance to see my x-rays. I saw that the bones were not lined up evenly. They were off-center.

My stay in that hospital changed my lifestyle. Where I was a meek character who did as I was told, I found out that I could now talk up and question a lot of things that were going on. I started playing piano for the patients, sitting sideways, because of the cast on my leg; and the Red Cross, after a few weeks, gave me a broken Underwood portable typewriter that didn't work too well. They said that the typewriter was a present for playing piano for the patients.

I fixed that typewriter, and since I didn't play cards in the ward with the guys, I went to the library and got a book on typing and Gregg shorthand. To sum it up,

I copied all my records (which I still have), and now I had some information that I could use in the future. I decided to do some writing and figured I'd learn to type by writing the story of my furlough trip to New York and back. I titled it as "My 2,500 Mile Furlough Trip." By the time I finished the twelfth or thirteenth draft, I knew how to type. I sent the article to the *Enthusiast*, which is the Harley-Davidson periodical, and to the *Motorcyclist* magazine in California.

In October I wrote the *Harley* people and asked them about my story; and they sent me a check for thirteen dollars with a note saying that since I was a soldier in the army, they were sending me the money, even though my story was published in the *Motorcyclist* magazine. I wrote to that magazine and got a check for ten dollars. I made twenty-three dollars that month. I also have to tell you that then the base pay of a soldier was only twenty-one dollars a month.

We still had the apartment in Anniston, and I remember borrowing a radio from the Wetzels before the accident. Florrie would visit me almost every day, and I also had visits from the Wetzels. Then one Sunday, December 7, 1941, Richard asked for the return of the radio. I got a pass from the hospital, and we went to the apartment to get it. I said, "Let's see if it's still working."

It was 2:00 p.m., and when we turned the radio on, we heard that famous broadcast that Pearl Harbor was just bombed. Needless to say, we all ran back to the camp because they announced on the radio that all troops should return to camp immediately. I went back to the hospital, although they said that I didn't have to rush back. But it was a big turmoil with all the troops running around. About a week or two later,

Hi Babit

the whole Twenty-seventh Division was shipped out to the West Coast. Being in the hospital, I didn't leave with my outfit.

Near Christmas time, I got a furlough, and Florrie and I went back to New York before I had to return to duty with the band. I picked up my *Motorcyclists* magazine at Times Square, and I still have that copy. When we came back to Fort McClellan, we were put on a train to rejoin the division at Camp Haan, California. It took us about three to four days to go cross country through the southern states to get to Camp Haan.

When I got back to the band, I was told that I was being transferred to a line company, Company E, 106th Infantry. I never had any training while I was with the band, and I questioned it, but you know the army has its own way. We were shipped up to Fort Ord that weekend for our new place of residence.

Florrie kept traveling with me. We got an apartment in Monterey, which was the town near the fort. On the first day out from our tent area for maneuvers, I couldn't keep up with the troops. By the time we left the company street, I was walking alone, dragging after the troops. The band was laughing as I walked by, alone with my rifle and backpack. I guess I was the lone doughboy. After limping out a mile or two and seeing the lunch truck go by, I turned around and went back to the dispensary and told the doctor, Major Sirbu, that I couldn't keep up with the troops. I asked him about getting a job typing or playing organ for services, but instead he put me back in the hospital.

Florrie would visit me every day. Oh yes, I have those pictures. There was one incident when one of the young doctors came to me and asked me to go to the next wardroom with him. There he asked me to lie down on a gurney, flat on my back, and that I should gaze into the light that he put over my face. I thought I was back in the hotels where we would put on skits of make-believe hypnotism. I figured that I would go along with him and listen to him. He used the same phraseology, "Gaze into the light. Your eyes will close, and you will listen to me." Then he said, "When you wake up, you won't have no more pain." And I'm thinking, *Schmuck, that's a double negative.*

He snapped his fingers; and being flat on my back, I got up quickly, which made my head swim. I got off the gurney, held on to it, and started to wobble my way out of the room. I could feel him watching me limp back to my ward. My acting days in the Borsht Belt paid off.

I appeared before the CDD (Certificate of Disability Discharge) Board a few times. They, of course, asked me if I wanted to get out of the army; and I always answered them that I didn't want to get out, but why couldn't they give me a job I could do? I wonder what would have happened if I did say that I wanted to get out of the army? I don't remember how many times I went before that CDD Board. They would show me the x-rays and would make the remarks that my healing was like a good plumbing weld of the bones. But you could see that the bones were not evenly mated. I didn't want to say that it was a bad weld. After all, I did know how to weld.

Then they sent me to Letterman General Hospital in the presidio of San Francisco. We found an apartment in Frisco and did a little sightseeing around town. I believe I even rented a car, and we took a trip up to someplace called the Twin Mountains. I went before some CDD boards there, and they finally decided to send me to O'Reilly General Hospital in Springfield, Missouri.

Now I have a problem getting Florrie to come with me. I went to the transportation officer, and he said not to worry, that she was a refugee from Pearl Harbor. She came on the same hospital train that I was on; and after a couple of days, we were in Springfield, Missouri.

I went looking for an apartment, and after finding one, I asked the landlady if there was a JWB in the area. She asked, "What's a JWB?" And I explained that it was a Jewish welfare board. She then asked, "Are you Jewish?" When we said we were, she then asked, "Where are your horns?" You may laugh, but I heard from other people who were there in those days that it was the mentality of the people at that time.

I was probably in that hospital a couple of months, and they finally decided to send me back to limited-service duty. I was then transferred to Fort Leonard Woods, Missouri. We left the hospital on Thursday, May 28, 1942. It was the Memorial Day weekend. When we got to Waynesville, Missouri, I thought it looked like a western town with wooden sidewalks and buildings that looked like it was from a western movie. That was the local town for the fort. We got to camp, and I reported to Post-Headquarters Detachment to which I had been assigned.

Over the weekend with work details, someone in the barracks saw my typewriter and said that they were looking for typists in Post Headquarters. I went into Post Headquarters on Monday, June 1, 1942, and checked with Sergeant Herbst, the sergeant major, if he was looking for typists. I told him I had a typewriter in the barracks, and he asked if I knew anything about special orders. I said yes, and he sent me up to the second floor to the Special Order section. There were two nice Irish guys who were going to OCS (Officer Candidate School). They gave me a paper and asked me to type a copy on the new Underwood Electromatic typewriter. I typed what they gave me, and I became a member of that office. I learned that special orders were nothing more than movement orders, duty and promotion orders.

I was a private then. On July 1 I became a corporal, and August 1, I became a sergeant. By that time I was already running that office, and because I had to run secret-movement orders, I was taking over some other offices. By December I became a staff sergeant. I had my own room in the barracks. I never stood for reveille or retreat for the rest of the war. It seemed like I was a civilian worker in the army. I got away with murder, as the expression goes.

I rented a trailer for us so that Florrie was on the base with me. That summer Florrie became pregnant, and she went home to Brooklyn in the fall of 1942. I went home a few times to visit before my daughter Laurie Gail was born on March 22, 1943, in Manhattan, New York.

I mentioned previously that when Florrie went to New York in June of 1941, I wrote a song, "Away from You." I rewrote the middle part of the song after the war started when I knew I couldn't get out at the end of my one year's service. I think that song would still be current today. The words in the middle part of the song can still be referring to today's army involvement all over the world. I'll phrase those words first with the original middle, and then with the later middle part. The first, "I left you back in our hometown, I thought I'd be back soon. The days go by, I wish that I, could just be back home with you"; the second version is, "I left you back in our hometown, I thought I'd be back soon, but now that I've a job to do, I won't be back till it's through, and on that day, when I will be home to stay . . ." What do you think? Would it be current today with our troops away all over the world? Incidentally the cover drawing of "Away from You" was made by a Japanese-American soldier. How I met him, I don't remember. But you can tell from the drawing that the artist was Asian. I still have the original cover drawing in color.

    I tried to get my family to come out to the camp where I had the trailer, but there was a problem with Laurie's health, and I was told that they couldn't travel. So I gave up the trailer and took trips to Brooklyn. Florrie lived at her mother's house on Lefferts Avenue while I was in the army.

    I felt like a civilian worker because I'd get up in the morning, make my breakfast in the mess hall, and then go to post headquarters to work. I became a Tech Sergeant in the spring of 1943 and was beginning to take over all the duties and offices in headquarters. They finally made me the Post Sergeant Major. They never gave me the master sergeant rating for the position of post sergeant major because of the TO, which I think stood for the table of organization, concerning ratings.

I did do a lot of piano playing in the service club, which was situated across the road from Post Headquarters. Sometimes I would stay later at the office if there were things that had to be attended to. If I didn't stay late at the office, then I'd be at the service club playing piano for the boys. At times I was asked to play at the nearby towns of Rolla, or Lebanon, with a dance band. Once in a while I would fill in with a USO group that came in. I have a photo of Jose Iturbi's sister Amparo and me playing the piano in that service club.

Another interesting anecdote occurred in my office. I have to explain that officers going on leave had to have copies of their leave orders for them to be able to buy liquor. One day a second lieutenant came to my desk and, with a gruff command, demanded ten copies of his leave orders. The way he said it turned me off. Had he asked nicely, I would have given it to him, but he riled me, and I said "no way," that he was only entitled to two copies. He said he would go to the adjutant, and I directed him to that person. The adjutant told him that whatever the sergeant major says is what goes on. While waiting for him to come back, I noticed that on the request, his name was Lieutenant Fierst, theater officer.

Well, Florrie's brother Joey was a motion picture operator in the New York theaters. The union Joey belonged to took in only family members. I thought when I got back to civilian life that I would like to be a movie operator. When the lieutenant returned, I asked if he was the theater officer. When he said yes, I said that I would give him any amount of leave orders on one condition. I told him that I wanted to learn how to run the projectors in the movie house. He said OK. I became a motion picture projectionist. Something else that I learned.

Fort Leonard Wood was not a small camp. It was an ERTC (engineer replacement training center); we had a German prisoner of war camp there, and we shipped divisions through that camp. They used some of the German POWs in the signal lab behind post headquarters for various chores, and I got some of those prisoners to do my photo developing and printing. It was crazy, but there were a lot of things you could do there.

I had the clout to give myself a pass to go visit my brother before he was shipped overseas to England. I went to see him at Camp Lee, Virginia. I was carrying a .45 gun all because I had just delivered a prisoner to Atlantic City. I think I did that twice. Once was to visit with him, and another after I delivered the prisoner, I went home to Brooklyn to see Florrie. It was a joke being a guard because they gave me a .45 with no clip in it. I was usually taking a hospital patient that was a prisoner to the Chalfonte Hotel in Atlantic City, which was then an army hospital, but you know it now as the Resorts Hotel and Casino. I think that I took two or three prisoners to that hospital

I got a fast pass to visit Rube when he was in the hospital in January of 1943 in Omaha, Nebraska. Rube says that he still has all those photos of my visits with him. I took the photos and gave them to him. I visited him in Camp Ellis, Illinois and also Rockford, Illinois.

I think it was about the fall of 1944 that my company commander from the post-headquarters detachment came into headquarters one day and asked me, "Sergeant, can you do me a favor and go out to the firing range so that I can put on your service record that you fired a rifle." It was not an order but a request. So I took the time off, put on some work clothes—my fatigues—and went out to the firing range and got a marksmanship medal. As I said before, I never had any formal army training, but I seemed to impress my superiors that I could really fire a gun.

When the war drew to a close in fall of 1945 and the point system was used for the discharges of the soldiers, I was told that I couldn't get out then because they needed me! When the commanding officer went on a trip west, I went to the hospital and got my CDD discharge. That was October 18, 1945. I was now a civilian, and I went home to Brooklyn, New York.

Chapter 4

The Years 1946 to the Present Time

I came home to 299 Lefferts Avenue where Florrie had been living with our daughter, Laurie Gail. We lived in my mother-in-law's house until my mother bought a house for us at 2448 Bedford Avenue, between Cortelyou and Clarendon avenues. I think we moved to the new house in early 1946. It was a nice two-family house, and we lived on the second floor. The previous owner had lived on the lower floor, and when they moved out, we had an apartment ready for a new tenant.

We had been using a dentist who was treating my sister-in-law Sylvia Goldsmith and me and Florrie. When I mentioned to him one day when I was there that we had an apartment for rent, he said that he'd be interested in getting it. I asked him why, and he answered that he was tired of owning a house and taking care of it and that he'd rather rent. It seemed like it was a nice deal. However, a couple of years later, things changed. I'll tell that story later on.

One of the first things I did was to buy a piano. I found an old upright piano that had been a player piano. The guts of it were already removed, and of course, this was before I got involved with making player-piano rolls. It was a Kranich & Bach piano that had a great tone. This is why I bought it. It was a tall upright, about fifty-four inches high, and years later I tried another of my inventive ideas with it. I will explain.

In the '40s and '50s. the piano dealers started to take old uprights and redesign them to look smaller in height by cutting down the top front of the piano and putting a mirror along the length so that it gave the illusion of not being as tall. The harp was still the same, but it didn't look as bulky or boxy and big. Should I use the word "illusion"?

In the late 1950s or early 1960s when high fidelity became a big marketing project, I decided to do something with my piano. I had a Sano accordion and a Sano amplifier. I was experimenting with sound because of the new wave of high fidelity that was coming out. This was before stereo. I accidentally figured out how to get a stereo effect when I began my experiments. I had a Grommes ten-watt amplifier and a Bogen Lenco turntable. The Grommes amplifier had radio tubes and not transistors and therefore was able to produce a loud sound.

I cut down the top of the front of the piano at a forty-five degree angle. I took off the front board and made a new shelf for the sheet music. I cut two oval-shaped holes with one at each end of the shelf. Then I cut a notch for two slim fluorescent bulbs in the front center of that music shelf. I took out the sliding door from the bottom board that opened and closed for the foot pedals when it was a player piano. Don't forget, this was an old player piano without the guts. It was now just a regular piano. My idea was to make a big speaker of that piano by installing speakers and connecting it to my amplifier and turntable. I did not intend to amplify the piano but only to use it as a big speaker. I got surprising results.

I went to a war-surplus radio store and bought five speakers. I bought one large twelve-inch speaker, two eight-inch oval speakers, and two three-inch small speakers, which I think were called "tweeters." That was the era of a lot of high-fidelity shows. I asked the radio-store person about getting the device that was called a "crossover" to separate the highs from the low sounds, and he sold me two condensers for thirty cents each; those crossovers, at the hi-fi shows, cost about twenty-five dollars. My five speakers cost me only about twenty dollars. The twelve-inch was eight dollars; the eight-inch oval speakers cost about four dollars each, and the two three-inch tweeters cost about two dollars each. I'm not a sound expert, but I was just trying out and experimenting with some ideas. I bought two volume controls and two fluorescent thin bulbs. I was told how to wire up the five speakers.

On the front folding lid, where the player controls used to be, in front of the playing keyboard, I placed three volume controls and a light switch. I mounted the two thin light bulbs on the music shelf and also mounted the two oval speakers at each end of that music shelf. I took the foot-treadle door, cut a round opening in it, and mounted the twelve-inch speaker. At the top of the harp, I mounted the two tweeter speakers with about four feet between them. I drilled a hole in the bottom board for an acoustic line jack that would run from the amplifier to the piano. Now I was ready to try my experiments with making the piano a big speaker. I figured it would have a great sound.

This was the time when the LPs were a big seller. Remember those LPs were only monaural records. My piano was on the east wall of the room. My Sano amplifier was on the west side of the room. I boosted all the bass on the Sano amplifier and turned off the treble sound. I boosted all the treble on the piano controls and cut the bass sound. I ran a wire from the Sano amplifier to the Grommes machine and ran a wire from the piano also to the Grommes. I had a "y" connector to the Grommes from the piano and the Sano. I put a record on the Grommes and started the music. What a sound!

Believe it or not, I was getting stereo effects. You heard the lows from the Sano and the highs from the piano. The piano itself was a huge speaker. After all, the soundboard of a piano amplifies the sound of the strings. Imagine what it does for the music records! As for the top lid of the piano, I bought tapered legs and made a cocktail table out of it. I used red-devil paint remover to remove the old varnished look of that piano and found beautiful cherry mahogany underneath. I left the Kranich & Bach logo on the underside of that coffee-table lid. With a little bit of polish, I had a nice, functional coffee table.

When stereo came out as a new big item years later and I saw some of the new stereo LPs with its contents, I laughed about some of the selections. For instance, they had a stereofied LP of Benny Goodman at the 1938 show at Carnegie Hall. There was no stereo in 1938. Now I knew how they got that stereo effect—separate the highs and lows on two channels. So again, you can fool the people with gimmicks.

The basement of my house had an oil burner at the back end of the house, which left a long empty space for doing something, and since I liked to build things, I decided to build two rooms for my pet projects. I built two rooms, a woodworking room and a photography room. I've always had cameras. First I started with a box camera. Then I got an Argus C3 35mm camera, which I used from before World War II to the 1960s. So the photography room was a necessary one for me to be able to develop pictures. Later on I acquired a Minolta 35mm camera with an F1.4 lens. I used that camera in my flying years. It was a great camera for taking sunset photos and night shots of the New York City area from the air, when you were allowed to fly over New York at night. I also acquired two View-Master cameras for 3-D work. I will talk about those projects later on. The woodworking room was for the projects I made.

I've carried boxes of negatives with me for years. I've had them during the years of my first and second marriages. When I got my second XP computer, I found that I could print photos from those negatives. I had to learn the tricks of the "new" way of printing photos. I made albums for my daughter and the other families. They were happy to get all those '30s and '40s pictures. The new way was a far cry from the old way of developing film.

The old way of developing negatives was to use a darkroom to put the film into a developing tank in the dark. Then with the light on, you could feed a solution into the tank for developing. When the process was finished, you hung the 35mm filmstrips up to dry. Then we used enlargers to crop and blow up the photos to whatever size you wanted. You tried to get the best results. The paper prints were developed in solutions, and then you either hung up the photos to dry or you used electric dryers. I did like the old way of doing photography, and while I did have better ways and control of making prints, I must admit that it was quicker and easier to use the computers and much cleaner. There were no liquids, no fuss, and no muss. It was all dry work.

I worked in my father's factory during the week. On weekends, I played club dates with bands. I had the new Solovox that was attached to a piano, and it could sound like an organ. I used it for weddings and other affairs. Not having a car, it was hard to drag the whole set on the subway or trolley car (they were still running in those days), and it sure was a bit much.

I started playing USO shows in 1946 and did the USO shows for about ten years. At first we traveled around the Eastern United States. I did the tours along the northeastern and the southeastern states. I played piano on most of those early tours. In the early '50s I may have brought my accordion on some shows. We did mostly hospital appearances. Some of it was not exactly conducive to smiling and laughing, because some of the hospitals, like the Greenbrier in West Virginia, had a lot of basket cases of soldiers. We had to smile and make merry. You felt more like crying.

In Fort Benning, Georgia, I ran into some high brass that I remember playing for when I was stationed in Fort McClellan, Alabama, and when I asked them about my old division of the Twenty-seventh, they just shrugged and said that those troops were used mostly for the Pacific beachheads landings. That meant that very few of them came back. That's why I say that my motorcycle accident in 1941 saved my life because when I rejoined the band in Camp Haan, California and I was transferred to a rifle company, I don't think that I would have ever made it back to the USA. So I've always believed in "destiny." The Jewish word or Hebrew word for "destiny" is "basherrt." I've had so many close calls in my life that I firmly believe in "basherrt." When my time is up, whether I like it or not, it will be up. My advice is to live and enjoy life! As the saying goes, you only live once!

On some of those show tours, we had little sleep and traveled long hours. One trip was from New York to Fort Erie, which is almost into Canada and situated north of Buffalo, New York, at the tip end of New York State. We got there in the evening, set up, did the show, and started our return trip about midnight. When we got back to New York City the next morning, the agent had us going down to Fort Dix in New Jersey for a show that night. What troupers!

Another trip that was memorable started at Floyd Bennett Field in Brooklyn, which was then a navy base. We were flown in a DC-3 to Newport, Rhode Island, where they put us on a PT boat and motored across the bay to an island. We did the show at a hospital there, and they flew us back that same night to Brooklyn. It was a great trip.

On one of the tours to the northeast to Fort Winthrop near Boston and to Fort Devens in the middle of

Massachusetts, we had a hypnotist in the group. His name was Dr. Arthur Ellen. He did a good act of hypnotism. Dr. Ellen lived in Brooklyn, and when we got back after one of our tours, he invited the group to his house for a little get-together. It was not often that we did that. Usually after a show, we all went our different ways. Also in the troupe was the director, who was also the comic, and he was Jackie Wakefield. He did a lot of shows all over the country, and occasionally I would work with him. I believe that when I first moved to Florida, I went to see him at a local show in Fort Lauderdale. I went backstage, and as usual we talked about the good old days.

Dr. Ellen, or Arthur, called me aside when we were in his house and mentioned that he had a mail-order business of music lessons. When I asked him what he knew of music, his reply was, "Nothing." So I asked to see what he was selling. He brought out a package with a book and a long cardboard piano keyboard with names on the keys in it. You put the cardboard keyboard behind the same keys of the piano. The white keys had a number on it, and the black keys also had a number plus an "x" on it. For instance, the white key "F" had the number "1" on it. The next white note "G" had the number "2" on it. Therefore the black note "F Sharp or G Flat" had the number "1X" on it. I think you get the idea. The book did not have music notation but had the title of the song, such as "Way Down upon the Suwanee River," and instead of notes it had numbers, such as 2, 1, 5x, 5, etc. If you followed those instructions and hit the corresponding number and letter of what was in the book, then you could somehow play the song,

When I asked him how the student would know the way to play the correct rhythm to get the right sound of that song, his answer to me was, "Let them play the song the way they sing it." Is this how to learn music? But he said that he had a good business going. How about that? What was that phrase about fooling people all of the time?

In the summer of 1947 and 1948, I again played at the Kenmore Hotel in Livingston Manor. This time I brought my wife and daughter to enjoy some of the summer there. I have some photos of Laurie in a rowboat on our little lake and also on the activity fields. If I remember right about that time, Florrie came on weekends and went back to the city during the week to work. Sometimes she brought her sister Rosie up for the weekend.

The entertainment director and comic was Hy Sands who became well known in later years for fund-raising events. In 1948, the Kenmore had a fire in one of the buildings. I think that the two top floors of one of the buildings were gutted. I went to the little airport in Livingston Manor; rented a plane, a piper cub, and pilot; and then flew over the hotel to take photos of that gutted building. I liked flying and photography!

I mentioned Buffalo before, and I want to say that I took Florrie and Laurie up to visit Eileen Wetzel in Williamsville, which is a suburb of Buffalo. This was long before I went there to make piano rolls. We found out that her husband Richard was killed in Okinawa by a sniper, just before he was to return to the United States. After the war, his sergeant, Bill Snow, came to visit Eileen; and shortly after, they got married. Now we traveled to Buffalo to visit them. I'm guessing that it was the early '1950s. I think I had the View-Master camera then, and I used it to take photos of a trip to Niagara Falls and the area. Sometime later, maybe a year or two, I had occasion to visit with the View-Master company in New York and showed them the photos that I took of Niagara Falls; and they seemed impressed and said that my photos had better composition than theirs. I was flattered.

This was before the thruway was built, and we had to take the old Route 17, and then Route 20. It was quite a trip, and we stayed overnight in an old-fashioned motel. The names for those places might have been called either tourist cabins or motor courts. Take your pick. While traveling on Route 17, about an hour north of Roscoe, New York, we got pulled over for speeding (but we were not speeding) by state troopers who made us follow them to a little town with a one-legged judge. The troopers wouldn't answer our questions. The judge just wanted the ten-dollar fine, or he would throw us in jail because we questioned the ticket. Florrie argued with the judge and he kept threatening to jail us, so we paid the fine and went on our merry way. There used to be a burlesque skit for a similar situation where the punch line was, "Pay the $2.00 Sam!"

In later years when I made piano rolls for QRS and traveled to Buffalo to make them, I would stay at the Snow residence and even used one of their cars to go to the factory. Once in a while, Florrie and I would stay at a motel instead of at the Snows. I remember staying at one of the motels where I started playing piano at their restaurant and ended up getting a free stay there because of my piano playing. I usually made tape recordings of my playing in various places and just have to look and listen to a lot of my old tapes to find out which ones are for the places that I've played at.

There was the time that Florrie and I went to Montreal, Canada, and then we extended our vacation by making an extra trip to St. Jovite, which is about seventy-five miles north of Montreal to the Grey Rocks Inn, which was a hotel in the Laurentians. I wanted to go there because in my AOPA *Flying* magazine, I always saw an advertisement for an invitation to fly in to the Grey Rocks Inn airport in St. Jovite. When we were approaching that hotel, I saw that the airport had the most beautiful grass landing field that I had ever seen. It was like a green carpet.

The hotel had vista looking areas of the Laurentian mountains that were like the ones you see in the movies or magazines. I think we were there about a week. They had a band there, and when I came to listen, I saw a Hammond organ standing idle, and I asked the leader if I could sit in with the group. I ended up doing a lot of playing and recording there. Now if I could only find the tapes. It seems that no matter where I traveled, I always end up playing piano.

I'm going to jump ahead to the present time to augment that blurb about ending up playing piano. In 2008, my sister Roz asked me if I would like to go to her granddaughter's wedding in Holyoke, Massachusetts. I would ordinarily say no, but she suggested that we spend a couple of days at the Mohegan Sun Hotel and Casino in Connecticut before we went to Holyoke. I said OK because I liked the idea of going to a new casino. Well, we went to the Mohegan on Wednesday,

The Flying Piano Roll Man

and my daughter came up Friday to pick us up and take us to Holyoke.

Saturday night was the wedding. I was supposed to be a guest. We got there, and I saw that they had a guitar player on stage and a setup for a band on that stage. I sat at the table and watched the guests. My nephew came to me about an hour later and asked if I would do him a favor and play piano for a few minutes and give the guitar player a break. I said that the piano was closed, but he had them open it. Roz came with me; and while I thought I would play about ten minutes, with Roz feeding me numbers to play, I did play for about an hour or more. Sometimes I call Roz my shill.

I finally said "enough" and got a standing ovation. I laughed and went back to my table. The band played, and the guests danced. I sat and watched. About an hour later, my niece came and asked me to do her a favor and go up and play "Hava Nagila" and a tarantella. I asked her, "Doesn't the band know how to play those," and she said they didn't. I got up and played those numbers for the guests to dance to, and then sat down. When the wedding was over and the people were leaving, they all stopped at my table to tell me that I made the evening pleasurable. I laughed and thanked them. So here was another night that I got involved in entertaining.

Speaking of, the Canadian trip reminded me of another trip that Florrie and I took to visit Canada. We always liked to see the autumn colors in the New England area and planned a trip to the Canadian province of Quebec. We went by way of Vermont and New Hampshire; we visited the "old man of the mountain area" when it was still there. Then we went to stay at the Chateau Frontenac in Quebec City. It was a delightful trip. I tried out my fractured French, and they did not want to talk to me. But when we took a side trip east of the area and came to a little island with a church, we had fun because they wanted to practice talking English to us.

When I was married the second time, I again wanted to go to Canada and revisit those same places, but it wasn't the same as the first time. We did go to the Thousand Islands and Fort Henry in Kingston, Canada. We traveled east to Quebec from Kingston and visited the Chateau Frontenac, but it changed. Then we traveled down through Maine to go back via the Boston area to New York, but although we enjoyed the trip, it didn't have the same taste as before.

My airplane logbook shows that I flew out of Liberty and Wurtsboro airports for the summers of 1964 and 1965. I started my memory banks to work again to remember where and when. I did play in 1964 at a hotel that was behind the Pines Hotel in Fallsburgh. A few years later, that same hotel became the helps' quarters for the personnel of the Pines Hotel. It happens that my father passed away July 3, 1964, and I had to leave the July 4th weekend, playing to go back to Brooklyn for the funeral. I can't remember the name of that hotel.

In 1965 I played at the Young's Gap Hotel. That hotel was on Route 17 between Liberty and Parksville. It was a swinging place noted for its young and not-so-young singles. I see in my logbook that I did take a lot of the guests and friends flying from Liberty airport.

I played again at Klein's Hillside Hotel in Parksville for the summers of 1966 and 1967. That was about thirty years after the first time playing there in the '30s. While at Klein's Hillside Inn, I did a lot of flying at the Liberty airport, also known as the Grossinger airport, because it was just behind that hotel. After Labor Day in 1967, I played as the show pianist at Kutsher's Country Club in Monticello for about three to four months. In 1968 I played for one summer season at Ackerman's Hotel in Mount Freedom, New Jersey. That was the summer I did a lot of flying at the Morristown airport and for the Civil Air Patrol there.

I know I'm jumping around over the years, but I'd like to go way back to the time I lived on Bedford Avenue in Brooklyn and explain about the trouble that my tenant gave me and my wife. One reason is that if I did not have that trouble with my tenant, destiny might have moved a different way. I wouldn't have had to sell the house because of all that trouble, and life might have been different. My tenant, Dr. Irving M. Gurland, started his shenanigans about two or three years after he moved in. I started getting summonses to appear in magistrate's court for put-up excuses, like closing the basement door and not allowing the tenant access. The trouble was that Gurland would put wood filler in the lock so that even I couldn't open it. At another time, he drilled a hole from his bedroom floor and dropped garbage through it into the cellar, and then called the Health Department to come see the garbage.

I lived on the top floor, and the tenant lived on the lower floor. There was one time that he called me down to see something that was broken, and when I came into his apartment, he had his wife call the police. He locked the door, but I got out of the front window.

The police were called often, and they began to see that he was causing a lot of trouble, but they tried to stay out of it.

I was starting to become a regular visitor to the magistrate's court on Snyder Avenue. I had to hire a lawyer named Gittelson, and he would come late or adjourn a date just the same as Gurland would do. I started to keep records of all the court appearances and adjournments. It came in handy later when I found out that Gurland was trying to get my house for nothing by way of legal trickery or chicanery. I couldn't throw him out because they had those rent control laws then. Gurland had a dental office built Downtown Brooklyn on Lafayette Avenue opposite the Brooklyn Academy of Music. Then I found out that his wife called police one day, because they found him in the office with gas coming out of the jets. I understand they took him to Kings County Psycho Ward on Clarkson Avenue. He tried to sue Brooklyn Union Gas Company for bad construction that led to the broken gas incident. He also sued Con Edison for some of his made-up problems. His stay at that institution also saved me and Florrie from a court incident later on.

I also found out that Gurland didn't get a certificate of occupancy (CO) for his dental office because he would break things. Since he didn't have the CO, he didn't have to pay any bills to the builders of his office building until there was a valid CO. What a conniver.

He finally got a summons against Florrie and me for assault, battery, theft, etc. Since my so-called lawyer wasn't doing much except giving me bills, I had to become a detective and find out things for myself. I went to the newspaper morgue of the *New York Journal* and found out about his stay at the Kings County Psycho Hospital in Brooklyn after that dental office gas incident. He and his wife were also involved in fake automobile-insurance accident claims. As a detective, I had to track down all kinds of information and find the results. I learned the hard way how to investigate. This was necessary for survival!

One time Gurland came into magistrate's court and said that he was major or colonel in the army. He was wearing half a uniform, so I called the FBI, and they came to court and arrested him. I had a hunch and asked Florrie to take a trip with me to Governor's Island to ask if he had been given a commission. At the hospital there they told me that he had gotten a lieutenant colonel commission the week before. I then showed them the records that I had kept of all his shenanigans and warned them what he would do to the poor soldiers. The next time in court, Gurland got up and began shouting to the court that I got him court-martialed and thrown out of the army. Needless to say, everyone in that court applauded me.

Florrie and I were up against a special sessions court with the old mayor Impelliteri. When I brought out the evidence of all Gurland's shenanigans, the case was dismissed, and we were free to go. But because of all that harassment, I went and sold the house. The new owners were also harassed by Gurland, and the house was sold again. The new owners and I think the police finally got him to move out of there. He moved to an apartment building about ten blocks north of that house, and I found out that he started doing the same things there.

My friend Mac Rubin came through and offered us an apartment at 152 Clarkson Avenue. We moved there about 1952. Florrie went to work for the city in Downtown Brooklyn. Laurie went to school on Rogers Ave. I was still doing club dates, and I think I was working for my father. I also had a nailhead business in my father's factory putting nailheads on ladies' coats. Nailheads are metallic stamped pieces that you put on clothing or leather belts to make it look different. I had the stamping machines on a table in my father's factory and I made designs for my customers products. It lasted a few years until the fad died.

I'm trying to remember the year that I got involved with making photos for a musician friend. I think that the year was about 1949. He knew that I could copy and print photos and talked me into making photos for a good price. The photos happened to be pornographic. I got a little apartment in New York City, and I bought some equipment. A fifteen-dollar Federal enlarger, out-of-date photo paper, some big 14 × 17 developing trays, a paper cutter for sizing those outdated photo paper to playing card size, and I was producing about two thousand pictures a day. I had figured out a method to do those big quantity photos. I had two big dryers to quickly dry the photos. You overlook risks when the money is good.

I bought a .45 Harley-Davidson motorcycle, and I started out to deliver two thousand five hundred pictures to a client in Scranton, Pennsylvania. My first day out on that motorcycle was to deliver those pictures. I left New York and went through the Lincoln Tunnel and started down the hill toward the west. It was a misty day, and I hadn't ridden a bike for ten years. I was used to a car where you step hard on the brakes. I had to slow up, and I guess I hit the brakes a little too hard. When I turned my head to see who was behind me, I must have taken a fast spill and never had the sensation of falling.

I found myself standing next to a fence, and a policeman was asking me if I was OK. I realized that in my saddle bags were all those photos, and if he saw them, I'm in trouble. He wanted to take me to a hospital, and I had to go. They thought I had a concussion, but I insisted that I wanted to go home to Brooklyn to see my own doctor and that I'd be OK. So the policeman took me back to the bike. I took my package, and I sat in the police car while he took me to the Holland tubes. I went home, and I was happy that I didn't get caught. That was the end of my photo work, and that was the end of my motorcycling days. I cracked up twice, and I wasn't going to try for a third one.

While all the shenanigans were going on, I didn't stop working. I was still doing music on weekends or whenever and also going to work in my father's factory. Working for him, I could get off anytime.

In 1949 I met another musician, Dinney Dinofer, and started to work for him both for club dates and also for a summer job that lasted about five years. In 1950 we started playing at Sains Hotel in Mount Freedom, New Jersey. That was a resort area about ten miles west of Morristown, New Jersey. We played there every summer until 1954. While I was at Sains Hotel, I did some more inventions. I invented trestles for model railroads and a four-handed checker game and even wrote a song.

First I will talk about the checker game. I first made an involved multiple four-handed game to include not only a checker game but also a chess game, scrabble, a math game, etc. I made a giant board with too many squares, and then realized it was a bit too much. I then made a simple checkerboard designed for four hands. I first called it Foresees because it had four different checkers in four colors, four players, and the word "Foresee" to imply that you have to foresee each movement. Then I named it 4-Cs, but there was that bread-crumb can marked 4-C. I made a nice board and made a trip to Providence, Rhode Island, to the Hassenfeld Bros. factory to show them my new game. We played for about six hours, and they said they would look further into it. I went back to Mount Freedom. Years later that company changed its name to Hasbro. About a year after my visit to their factory, they sent back the game, saying there were a few more games that came out similar to mine; so they said forget about it.

The game was dormant for years. I only showed it once in a while. It was about 1975 when I showed it and played it again. This came about because Dinney Dinofer got me a job as music director on a cruise ship for the July 4 sailing of the SS *Victoria*. I had gotten married to my second wife, Marilyn, in 1975; and we had a two- or three-day honeymoon at the Grossinger Hotel in Upstate New York. When Dinney called me and offered me the job, he said that I had to take my wife and pay two hundred fifty dollars for a two-week cruise in the Caribbean. I called Marilyn and told her. She thought it would be nice since our honeymoon had been so short.

The Flying Piano Roll Man

Since I just brought up my second marriage, I want to clarify things. I married my first wife, Florrie, in January 1941. We were married for thirty-three years, and she passed away from cancer in 1974. I married my second wife, Marilyn, a year later. We were married for thirty years, and she too passed away from cancer in 2005. I think I've set the record straight. Now back to the cruise.

Originally we were supposed to sail from New York City on Friday, but I got the call on Thursday night and was told that the ship had broken down in San Juan, Puerto Rico. The new plan was to go to Kennedy Airport Friday evening and meet the band. All the passengers were to be flown on two DC-10s from Kennedy to San Juan. We were already packed, and I included my checker game to kill time on board when we were not playing music. I also brought my piano-tuning tools in case I didn't like what the piano sounded like. It turned out to be a smart move.

We arrived in San Juan about midnight. We didn't get on the ship until about three or four o'clock in the morning. We were four men in the band, and I only remember the name of the sax player, and it was Harry Kolstein. When we got our staterooms, we found that it was not air-conditioned. Harry's stateroom also was not air-conditioned. He told me to follow him to the purser and to slip him ten dollars, and we both got upgraded to air-conditioned rooms and a higher level deck. Harry had been on cruises before, so he knew what to do for both of us.

I went looking for the ballroom and found the social director there. I was supposed to play the shows on board, and when I saw the piano, I knew we had trouble. I found an octave of keys below middle C was down and wouldn't play. When I asked the director about it, he said that they couldn't find a piano tuner in San Juan. I told him that he was lucky because I had brought my own set of tools, and he asked me if I could fix the piano, and I told him I could. I not only fixed that piano but I tuned and checked all the pianos on board that ship. When we finally got back to New York, I found out that I didn't have to pay for that trip.

I was told that I didn't have to play any shows because they had a flamenco group that was self-sufficient. They also had a young band from Boston playing opposite us. All we did was play dance music. I recently made a CD from some of the tapes I have of that cruise. We did play my checker game a number of times on board and had a lot of fun.

I have since redesigned the board and the checker and renamed the game to "Quads." It all came about when I took my grandson Richie, who was about six years old, to Las Vegas in 1986 for a karate competition. When I walked into Caesars Palace where we were staying, I noticed what the entrance floor looked like; my eye is always open for new things; I decided that was the design for my checkerboard. One of these days I'm really going to make some working models of that game and try it out in the condo where I live. Maybe something will come of it.

The game is very interesting and challenging, since it is meant to be played by four people as partners like in the game of bridge. Let me explain. I believe the game has the properties of bridge and chess. Why? When you play bridge, you hope that your partner will make the right move to help you win a game. It feels like chess, because you have to figure out each move. Basically it's a checker game where you move to the opposite side to get a king, but you have to watch out for your side opponents who can get behind you and get your checker. You cannot move back to take that opponent. It's not a five-minute game like ordinary checkers but a challenging game that takes longer to play.

The next invention was my trestle set for model railroads. When we lived on Bedford Avenue in Brooklyn, I would get a Christmas tree for my daughter and put a model train to run around it. One day when I was going to Sains Hotel in Mount Freedom, I saw something that got my invention mind working. I would sometimes take the subway to Manhattan then take the ferry from Forty-second Street to Hoboken, New Jersey, to get the Erie Lackawanna train to take me to Morristown, New Jersey, where I would take a bus to Mount Freedom. One day I was early on my arrival to the ferry building. I went up to the second floor of that building and was surprised to find a giant model-railroad setup that took up the whole length of the building. It took about ten people to work it.

I was impressed and got the idea of making a trestle set for the model trains to run around the Christmas tree. While riding in the train to Morristown, I observed all kinds of trestles and started to design something to make a prototype for what I wanted. I went to a patent office on Broadway and Thirty-second Street and had a search made. In those days, a patent search was only ten dollars. I wonder what the price would be today? I looked in all the model railroad magazines but found nothing similar to what I wanted. I started making my prototypes.

My father's factory was at 146 West Twenty-fifth Street. And A. C. Gilbert who made the American flyer model trains was at the corner of Fifth Avenue and West Twenty-fifth Street. There may be some people who don't know who A. C. Gilbert was. It was the company that made the old Erector and Chemistry sets. I went there and showed my prototypes to the model-train layout designer. He got very interested in my design. We worked on that design and improved it. One day I was told that A. C. Gilbert was interested in buying it. I forget the name of the fellow I was working with, but he told me that although A. C. Gilbert was very interested in getting my product; they would not pay royalties but would either buy it outright or steal it from me. I was advised to accept their offer of buying it rather than let them steal it.

I took the money, two thousand five hundred dollars, and as they say, I ran all the way to the bank. Everyone said that I was stupid for selling the idea and that I could have made a fortune. But I had the last laugh. I only worked on the device for six months and only had a patent application for it. I wish I could have done the same thing with my airplane invention, but I didn't follow through with the airplane device like I did with the trestle set.

I used one-eighth-inch cardboard for my trestle stands. When A. C. Gilbert came out with the device, they used the same type of cardboard; but they, being a big company, they came out with a plastic injection-molded unit that was nice; but for some reason they only made the device for their own track size.

The Lionel and Ideal companies copied the trestle-set idea for their gauge track, and they all ended up going to court. I was asked to go to court, but I declined. I was out of that game.

I would like to explain about the model trains. A. C. Gilbert made the American flyer train set, which was an S-gauge two-rail system. Lionel made an O-gauge three-rail layout, and the Ideal Company made an HO-gauge two-rail layout. HO meant "half of O" gauge, and those trains were smaller in size. All the companies ended up fighting each other in court. I was out of it. So I didn't have to fight anyone or go to court and spend money for lawyers. Ha-ha!

Incidentally, I acquired about eighteen engines, seventy-five cars, eighteen pairs of switches, and lots of railroad track. I have photos of the different layouts that I used to make every night before I sold the invention idea. I was running about three hundred feet of track within an 8 × 4 foot area. I wish I had those trains today. They should be worth a lot of money.

During one of the summers that I played at Sains Hotel in Mount Freedom, I composed a cha-cha song, which I put on a QRS piano roll, and it only stayed in the catalog about two years. The roll is QRS 9961. That song was composed because I had another habit of trying out counter-themes or obligato passages against what a sax or trumpet player may be playing. I liked to improvise those counter-themes instead of playing chords because it seemed so boring to just play chords. I used to get complaints of "Hey, Hi. Just play straight chords." It seems I threw them off with my improvisations and running around the piano keys.

There was a rumba that we used to play. You may remember the title "Magic Is the Moonlight." I first started to play a little phrase against that song. Then I began to augment the phrase, and soon I had a song that I called "But First, Let's Do the Cha-cha-cha." I wrote the words and began playing that song as a cha-cha with the bands. I didn't push it any further than just playing it until I made a piano roll in the sixties when I worked for the Imperial Company in the Bronx.

I did use that selection in one of the shows that I did a few years ago in one of our productions in our theater in Wynmoor where I live. I put that cha-cha roll on one of my CDs. It's not lost, but it's not in the public realm. So playing at Sains Hotel, I can count that I wrote a song there and had two inventions with a little bit of results.

Young musicians, especially on hotel jobs, had a habit of doing practical jokes. It seemed like fun to get into some trouble. At Sains Hotel, one summer (I don't know which year) Dinney bought a new tiny car called Crosley. One day or night (I forget) a group of us musicians took his Crosley and we carried it up and put it into the casino.

Dinney wanted to go someplace and he couldn't find the car, and of course we acted—concerned. He was ready to call the police and make a report, and we finally told him where the car was. At first he was mad and then he laughed about it. We always did a lot of practical jokes!

In 1955, Dinney got me a summer job at the Capri Theater in Atlantic Beach, Long Island, New York. There I met some of the movie and Broadway stars. Dinney gave me a photo showing me on the accordion,

Dinney with maracas, and Harry Frank on sax. We were playing for Sylvia Sidney, Menasha Skulnik, and Eva Gabor; we had other movie and stage actors and actresses at the Capri Theater. I played in the lounge for the guests between the acts. It was a nice summer job.

The following year, 1956, we went to Atlantic City for our summer job and played at the Breakers Hotel. The hotel was opposite the Garden Pier, which was across the boardwalk from the hotel. For those people who know or go to Atlantic City, the old Breakers Hotel was situated only a block from what is now the Showboat Hotel. My routine there was to have dinner at 6:00 p.m., and then go across the boardwalk to the Garden Pier at 7:00 p.m. to hear the Atlantic City Festival Orchestra. They performed there almost every night. I became friendly with the conductor of that group; and when our drummer, Bernie Kay, asked me to find out if he could sing with that orchestra, I got the OK. The orchestra had twenty-eight-players and needed musical arrangements for the singer.

I wrote out the arrangements and brought them over just in time for the 7:00 p.m. show. The conductor asked if it was safe to play without a rehearsal, and I advised him that it was OK. I had been studying orchestration with Siegfried Landau at the New York College of Music a couple of years earlier, and I was sure of the arrangement. At the end of the concert, the conductor said that he would play anything that I wrote. It was great for my ego. I was thankful for good instruction.

This was the first time that I used my orchestration ability for a real performance. So good instruction always pays off. Later on when I started making piano rolls, I did use those orchestration ideas for them.

I mentioned before about the New York College of Music, and I would like to expound about my time there. I wanted to use my GI Bill, from the Army days, to learn something. At first I wanted to take up flying, but I thought that I might lose my VA pension for the leg injury, so I decided to go with music. It was a wise decision.

I enrolled at the New York College of Music on East Eighty-third Street and Lexington Avenue in 1952 in Manhattan. In a way it was a joke because I already had about twenty years of show business behind me. Most of the students and teachers were very surprised and impressed that I could improvise and play like I did. I had a piano teacher named Ms. Clark, and she gave me some good material to learn. I had to learn the Mozart Piano Concerto No. 20 in D minor, and I also had to play the classical selections, like Schumann's Sea Pieces and Grieg's music.

I also studied orchestration under Siegfried Landau who was an orchestral conductor. He taught me how to write and orchestrate for all types of orchestras. He taught me how to write the music on the master score in the key of the different instruments so that when I had to copy the individual instrumental parts or scores, there was less chance of a mistake.

I was told that some composers wrote their scores in one key, usually in the key of C, and then when they had to make individual copies, they would have to transpose for each different instrument. Transposing invited errors.

I composed a four-hand arrangement of a Tarantella for two pianos, and that selection was used in some of their concerts. I also played on the radio station WFUV for the college and received good comments. I graduated in 1954 and went on with my music life.

I did some orchestration writing for some musicians to use with their acts, but then I stopped and just stuck to playing, piano tuning, and teaching. If I had to write orchestral arrangements now, I would have to restudy my old notes. I did use orchestral ideas for my piano-roll arrangements.

I learned how to play the accordion by teaching it. I had to stay one step ahead of my students. I laughingly say that I learned to read music and words upside down and backward because I would sometimes stand in front of the student and look down at the music on the music stand reading it upside down and backward. I also learned to play the organ by watching another organist friend of mine Larry Johnson. I always learned by watching and then doing. This applies also to when I learned to fly. Of course you know the saying that you learn by your mistakes. I watched, tried, made a lot of mistakes, analyzed, and learned.

In the fall of either 1951 or 1952, I began playing with the Hal Charm Orchestra at the Ansonia Hotel in Manhattan at Broadway and West Seventy-fourth Street. I think we played there on weekends, and it was for the Over 28 Club—a singles group. I was in the American band opposite the Latin band directed by Tito Puento. I will name one of the sax players in my band because his name is well known. Hal Linden played with me at the Ansonia Hotel for about three years. I still meet with Hal Linden once in a while when he comes to my condo to perform. He was a tall skinny kid then, and I have a photo of him behind me when we played the old Polo Grounds on Sunday afternoons for the football games. I was on the accordion with Hal on the saxophone.

Nowadays when we meet, we talk about who's left. Ha ha! I called him kid before because when he was here performing last March of 2009 at the condo where I live, I went backstage to see him. In the course of talking, he asked me how old I was; and after telling him that I'm turning ninety-two in November, I asked him how old he was, and he said that was turning seventy-eight the next day. So I can call him a kid.

I think we played at the Ansonia for about three years. When the Latin band came on, we would take our break. I would walk up Broadway, and one day I stopped at the corner of Broadway and Seventy-sixth Street at the Lighthouse Café. I heard an organ playing, and I could see the organist through the window. I stopped there often, and the organist one day motioned me to come into the café. He asked why I stopped there all the time, and I explained that I was playing piano at the Ansonia Hotel. He asked me to come up to the bandstand where he had a piano and asked me to sit in and play along with him. I did, and it became a regular routine. His name was Larry Johnson.

One day, a few months later, we went to a recording studio on Lexington Avenue, and made a demo record. We did what we call head arrangements. Either Larry would suggest a number or I would, and while we played, one of us would take the lead. It was spontaneous. That record is gone now, but I still have the tape, and I just made a CD of it. So it's not really lost. It's a bit scratchy, though. Larry and I thought that we could start a duo for future dates, but nothing came of it. Once in a while I'd run into Larry.

There was the time, years later, when I traveled to Reading, Pennsylvania, for the big International Air Show of the year, which took place every June in the 1960s and 1970s. Today the big International Air Show is held annually at Oshkosh, Wisconsin, at the end of July and the first week of August. I introduced my parking device for aircraft at the Reading Show in 1972. I would either drive or, when I belonged to the aero club and before I bought my airplane, I would rent a plane and fly there.

One day when driving back from Reading, I stopped in Kutztown, Pennsylvania for dinner. While I walked down the street looking for a place to eat in, I passed a restaurant and heard some organ playing. I listened and thought that there was only one person who played like that, and I walked in. Guess what? It was Larry Johnson. We talked, and I ate there, and then left. That was a nice surprise!

Most musicians have a style of their own. Larry had his style, I have my style, and no one style is better than another. It's all individual, and it's merely style! My style is because of my big hands and the use of my orchestration movements. I like to use moving tenths or sixths and a lot of scale runs and arpeggios.

I sometimes use the illustration or explanation by asking people if they have seen some magician's work. A magician seems to work or move so quickly and effortlessly to accomplish his show. In a sense I also feel like a magician and play quickly and easily. It's only an illusion. I run around the piano using scales and arpeggios, and I say that if musicians do what I do, they can also have a ball playing around with music. I think the trick is merely to add fill-ins, like scale runs or arpeggios, when the melody phrase ends and before the next phrase starts. There is always movement up and down the piano instead of just oomp oompa.

When I played at the Steak House in the Bronx, I spoke to people while I was playing. I had to keep playing, or the boss would say, "Stop talking and play." I was always improvising while I was talking to keep the sound of music going. Because of that, with all that improvising, I unintentionally composed songs. If I played something that sounded good, I'd have to do that phrasing about a dozen times or else it was lost.

Also sometimes when talking and playing, I would be asked about that nice selection I just played, and when I was asked what song it was, I said that I was playing nothing! I was only playing chord progressions in rythym and I would tell pianists that if you even played with your knuckles in rhythm, people would think you're playing something. It's an illusion!

I also want to add that I developed another crazy habit. You can get bored with the monotony of doing the same thing every day. Well, the organ had a light for the music stand, and I started—when it was slow and not too many people there—to look at my *Flying* magazines, which were always with me. I'd look at the photos, and little by little, I began to read the articles. Sometimes people would ask me how I was able to read while playing. I came up with the answer that I have a split personality or a dual personality, whichever fits. Ha-ha!

Watching how Larry used the drawbars on the Hammond organ, I merely copied what he was doing.

The Flying Piano Roll Man

The Hammond company had books of music with suggested numbers that were on the drawbars for the different music selections. What Larry Johnson did was much simpler and easier to get the sounds I like. So I used his style. I went out and bought a small spinet Hammond organ, and when I brought it home, Florrie asked why I bought an organ when we already had a piano. I tried to explain that one of these days I may get a job to play organ.

That's what happened in 1957. On the union floor one day, a musician friend asked me if I would like to bring my organ to a new restaurant in Yonkers, New York. This was about the Christmas season of 1957, and I said OK. The restaurant was called the Balalaika, and it was on the west service road of the Bronx River Parkway.

In case you are not familiar with the word "balalaika," it is a Russian instrument. It's a stringed instrument like a guitar, but the body is triangular shaped, and it comes in various sizes, like the violin family—from small to big bass sizes. They do have a unique sound, and once you get to hear those sounds, you will enjoy them. Some people think that it sounds like a mandolin. On the outside of that restaurant was a lit make-believe balalaika sign that must have been about twenty to twenty-five feet tall. You couldn't miss it when you drove up or down the Bronx River Parkway. I could recommend going on Google or YouTube and asking for balalaika vignettes. You will see and hear technique that will astound you.

We were a four-piece group. The leader was on trumpet, and his name was Sully Link. On the drums was Vinnie Camizzi; and on the sax, clarinet, and violin was Morty Ross. Both Vinnie and Morty alternated with singing songs. We played for the à la carte diners. It was a supper club, dining and dancing. After New Year's Eve, Sully decided he didn't want the job and asked if I would like to take over. I was always a sideman, or just one of the band members, and I thought that this was a chance to improve myself and become a band leader.

I would like to mention now, before I talk about the Balalaika job, that in the music business, I was always using the name Hy Babich. I did try to play with other stage names, even in the 1930s, where I thought of using the name Hy Babs; but I always stuck with Hy Babich. Musicians can be very funny or insulting at times, like they would greet me with, "Hello, Hy Babich, you old son of a bitch." We would laugh about it, but when I got the Balalaika job, I decided to really change my name and latched onto Hi Babit.

When I started to make piano rolls, I decided to use the name Hi Babit for the standard pop songs and to use my real name Herman B. Babich for the classical piano rolls. I did use my two names for making piano rolls, unlike J. Lawrence Cook, who used the name Sid Laney, or Dick Watson using the name Ted Baxter. When QRS came out with the "Boston Pops Medley," they took my three Leroy Anderson numbers that were on QRS single rolls and used three different names as the playing artists. When I questioned it, I was told that they wanted to show that they had a lot of arrangers, and they promised to put back my name on the medley box. But promises! They never did!

I have a lot of fun when calling customers about piano tuning and when I'm asked about my name and

I tell them or have to spell it out and mention that it's like the word "habit" but instead of an "h" you just use "b" and you have the name Babit. Then I add that, of course, "you can always make it a habit to call babit." They usually laugh and say, "Good! Use that saying." I laugh.

I would like to explain how I autograph the piano rolls. If you look at my signature on the roll, you will see that I sign it by capital "H," small "i," space, capital "B," small "a," capital "B," small "i," small "t." This highlights my three initials of "HBB." I did think that this would be a unique autograph.

I took over the Balalaika job and became a band leader. I called my group the Hi Babit Trio. I played both the organ and piano there. We did nicely. One day I happened to go downstairs to the basement, and when I looked at it, I went back up and spoke to the owners—Mike and Anne Beckish—about converting the basement into a catering place for weddings and parties. They liked the idea and fixed up the lower floor for catering. We turned from a supper club to strictly catering. I built up a nice following there. I once played a party for Gene Krupa and have a photo of the both of us. I played at the Balalaika for about seven or eight years before it was sold. I played hundreds of parties there.

My theme song while I was there was "At the Balalaika." That song was from a movie with Nelson Eddy who played a Russian and sang that song. I played there until someone by the name of Izzo came in and took over. When the new owners asked me to give them money for the privilege of playing there, I left.

I want to explain that the Izzos may have had a catering place; if I remember correctly, it was called the 1220 Club, because Izzo looks like 1220. Catering places were known to have house bands, which they would recommend to the prospective clients, and they would get a kickback from the band leaders for getting them those club dates. It was a well-known practice, but since I had built up the place for catering, I didn't feel that I owed giving the Izzos money. I went back to club dating at the union. I still had my teaching and piano tuning to back me.

In late fall of 1968, Dinney Dinofer recommended me to a job at Donaghy's Steak House Restaurant at West 230th Street and Broadway in the Riverdale section of the Bronx, New York. I passed the audition and started to play there. At first I had an old organ, and then I talked them into getting both a player piano and a newer Hammond organ. The company bought a Hammond XTP organ that had two speakers and a rhythm unit. I placed one of the speakers over the top end of the bar mirror-wall unit and placed the other speaker over the top of the coatroom. This way the audience could hear the organ playing throughout the whole restaurant. We also bought a player piano from Duffy's Store in Palisades Park in New Jersey. I had my *Stak-Raks* storage units behind me with my piano rolls. I was making good tip money since I knew which customer wanted me to put their favorite roll into the player piano and accompany the roll on the organ. It was a good gimmick, and I believe the only one in the world because I was the piano roll music arranger. I was there for only eighteen years.

While I was at Donaghy's, I was asked to appear on the Joe Franklin show on WOR-TV. I don't remember the date, but when I was there, he asked me to play live on the show since I didn't have any records for him to use. I played "Granada," and I have a tape of that show. I also had an early radio show that was played about 5:00 or 5:30 a.m., on which I advertised Donaghy's. The format for the show was of my flying and traveling to places in the U.S.A., and using the appropriate music for places. When it came to St. Patrick's Day, they advertised me as "Hi McBabit" and gave me a green yamulke to wear.

In the first couple of years, we had sing-a-longs almost every night. I learned a lot of Irish tunes, because the two bartenders were Irish tenors. They liked singing the semi-classical selections from the operettas of Victor Herbert, Rudolf Friml, and other writers. As the years went by, the crowd changed, and I changed my hours and nights there. I used my practical musical jokes according to the situations. For instance, one night while I was playing, some firemen came in and went to the kitchen in the back of the restaurant. I started playing the song "I Don't Want to Set the World on Fire." The manager came running over to me and yelled at me, "Are you crazy? Stop that!" I just laughed and changed the tune. If there was a party and someone started with taking pictures, I would start playing, "You Ought to Be in Pictures." I did try to liven things up with musical jokes.

Those years at Donaghy's were fruitful for a lot of reasons. I always improvised while I was playing, and in so doing I composed a lot of songs. There was another way to compose, and that was while I

Hi Babit

was driving from Brooklyn through Manhattan to the Bronx. I had a tape recorder on the passenger side of the car next to me, and while it took almost an hour to drive through New York City traffic to the Bronx, I would either compose songs or talk the lyrics to a tape recorder I had placed on the passenger seat next to me.

One of the songs I composed was "Dear Mr. Santa Claus." I thought that since every year the post office got a lot of mail from kids to Santa Claus, I should write a new song appropriate to that idea. I wrote that song and got a lot of year-round requests for it. I made a piano roll of that song, and it was in the QRS catalog for a couple of years, and then discarded. The number of that roll was QRS number 10-597.

I made some of the old style '45 records and sent them to all the DJ jockeys around the country, but nothing ever came of it. Some people remarked that I should have sent money or other recompense, but I didn't. I don't know if doing that would have helped. I did have visions of using that number for TV shows, school shows, and maybe also promoting toy units to sell with music sheets or singly. But, I had a lot of ideas and hopes.

I even tried to get it to some TV shows like *Little Webster*, but the agency turned it down saying they will decide what's good for their little star. I thought it would be an annual income for him, as well as for me, but they knew better. I met someone from Cherry Lane Music at Donaghy's and gave them some of my songs. I got royalties from Cherry Lane Music for only a couple of my songs. Mostly I got promises that they would do something with my songs, but all I got were promises. Maybe I should have given them "Dear Mr. Santa Claus."

Cherry Lane Music kept sending me statements with an amount of royalties that were due me. I was curious and called them one day to find out which song I was getting royalties for. After searching for the answer, I was laughingly surprised that the royalties were for the song "Away from You" that I wrote in the army in 1941. I don't know who performed it or when or where. I don't even know if I can find out. But I do think that it would still be an applicable number for our troops who are away in foreign countries.

I may be a bit old-fashioned in my songwriting, but I like to tell a story and have a good melodic line. I believe that today's songs rely on loud sounds and acrobatic antics on the stage and repetitive words that are monotonous. But that's my opinion.

I think it was in the sixties that I had a job playing at the Market Diner on West Fiftieth Street and Twelfth Avenue in Manhattan. My job was to come in to play at that diner when the Cunard Line ships came into port in New York. I had to watch the papers for the arrival dates. I had a lot of fun playing for those English sailors and learned a lot of English songs. My head library was increasing constantly.

I had the same experience of playing a lot of the "continental" restaurants in New York City where I had to learn the French, Spanish, Italian, Hungarian, Viennese, Russian, and various foreign music for the clientele. I played at a restaurant—Ken Later's "The Patio"—at the corner of Park Avenue and East Fifty-seventh Street. We were ten violins, and either I was on the piano or I was playing the accordion. The leader was a Russian called Gleb Yellen. He played piano, and I played accordion. When he wasn't there I played the piano. We had to wear white tie and tails. Customers were the crème de la crème of movie people and such.

The foreign songs that I learned to play came in handy when I did play private parties. If I heard people talking French, I would go into French music. Whatever language I heard, I would start playing that kind of music. The people were surprised that I knew those songs, and I made good tip money and got recommendations for more parties.

When Donaghy's bought a place in Mamaroneck in Westchester County, they asked me to play there. I had a console piano with a grand-style deck behind it where people could sit around and drink. I had a captured audience then, and when they asked me a question, I would answer them with a song. There are an unlimited amount of songs that you can use to answer a question. If you have a great knowledge of songs in your head, it will keep that tip cup filling up. People would laugh at my musical answers, and I had fun.

Playing at either restaurant, I would get requests for some songs that I would answer with the statement of it is not a good musical or piano number, and the retort to my statement was usually—"but it's got beautiful words", and I would always answer them "I don't play words, I play music". I've always said that there are a lot of songs that melodically make no sense. But, there are writers of songs that make money with nonsense.

Playing restaurants brings up a couple of stories of how I got involved with some other jobs. When I moved to Wynmoor in Coconut Creek, in 1996, Marilyn and I were driving on Powerline Road going home from someplace, and we passed a store marked "Danny's Pianos," and since I had never heard of him, I thought I'd stop in and inquire. When I told him that I was a piano tuner and mentioned about my piano rolls, he told me that he had heard about me, and would I like to tune pianos for him. That's how I got started with him. Danny rents out pianos, and he rented one to a restaurant in Delray Beach and gave them my phone number.

They called me and asked me about playing for them. I told them that I didn't play restaurants anymore. They asked me to please do them a favor and play at their place called Fratelli's for a few days until they could find a regular pianist. So I went there for a few days, and I stayed for about three years. When they got rid of the piano, because they wanted the table space, and gave me a keyboard to play on the counter near the front of the restaurant, I told them that I would stop playing because of the setup. I found another place, which is the next story. The next one was due to tuning and not to rental.

In an area called Wilton Manors, there is a Thai restaurant right on Wilton Drive that called me to tune a piano. When I got there, it was sitting on the outside, and I had to tune it with all the trucks going by and with all the street noise. I'm sure you know that a tuner needs quiet and not a lot of noise. After I tune a piano, I always play to make sure that it sounds good. While I played the owner came out and said, "You know how to play, and it sounds good. Would you like to play here?"

I told him that I was at another restaurant in Delray, but how many days and hours would he want me there. He told me he wanted someone to play three hours a night and every day. I gave him a price that was much higher than Fratelli's, and he said OK, and could I start that night. This was a few years ago when New Year's Eve came out on a Tuesday. This was on Monday when I tuned it. I went home, changed, and got back to the restaurant.

It was a great place for making tips, and I was there for about three or four weeks until the owner said that he had to let me go. I asked if something was wrong, but he answered that the people loved me. So why am I being fired? Like Fratelli's, he wanted the table space. That's restaurants. The people waited on line to get in, and I had a nice-tipping clientele, but they wanted the table space. Maybe that's what happened to live playing at most restaurants.

I think this may be the time to give my explanations of how I cured my stuttering and stammering. It's really a simple trick. I'm assuming that you have heard of some country singers who stuttered when they talked but never stuttered or stammered when they sang. That may clue you in to the answer. It's all in the breathing. If you take a breath before you say certain words that you can stutter on, you won't do it.

When I worked with Dinney Dinofer, he asked me to work in his office because in the New York area, he was one of the big band leaders. I didn't want to work in his office, because I knew that *D*s are the easiest letters to stutter on. I didn't want to answer the phones with "D-d-d-d-dinney Dinofer's office." Also when I started flying, I didn't want to go to airports with towers because I was afraid of being embarrassed.

For instance, I parked my airplane at Teterboro Airport in New Jersey for ten years. Sometimes I would call T-t-teterboro t-t-t-tower, and they would say, "Say again." The same problem was when I flew to Bu-bu-bu-buffalo. When I was running the band at the Balalaika restaurant, and I would have to use the mike to make announcements; I had to learn how not to stutter. I owe it all to the matter of breath control. This doctor's advice is learn to breathe before you say those types of words you can stutter on. That's free advice, so you don't have to go to any clinics.

I think I'll mention that I had a photo business of stereo. I had bought two View-Master cameras and their editing machine and their blank circular discs for putting the little slides in. I wrote an article and titled it "Selling without Samples" and mentioned my company name of Stereo by Hy. This article was published in the *Toys & Novelties* magazine of November 1952. I wrote about using the 3-D camera to sell a product that was too big to carry, like stoves, refrigerators, etc. That business lasted less than a year. I tried that idea, and it fizzled. But the next few businesses that I went into didn't fizzle.

Hi Babit, arranger for Q. R. S. Music Rolls.

Ramsi Tick meeting Hi Babit
at his airplane
in Buffalo, NY
1975

At the Balalaika
restaurant
1957-1966
Organ and Piano

AMICA '98, Niagra Falls, Can.
Hi Babit

"Looks like an old man!"

**In Boston for an
AMICA meeting
2007**

Playing at Coral Square Mall

Hi Babit "plays" some of his own rolls for comparison.
Convention 1998

Hi and Roz
Daily Companions
2010

Music Director - Hi Babit
For 1998 show at Wyndmoor

Hi Babit - piano, Mel Goldberg - sax,
Ted Kaufman - guitar, Herman Lang - bass, Harry Rubin - Drums

Hi Babit and Dinney Dinofer
at his office
1996

**Marilyn and Hi
about 2003
at Wynmoor Residence
with our car**

**Tuning a piano
Someone's home
2004**

Showing my
checker game invention called
QUADS
1997

Showing my Quads Checker game Board

Showing Tysafe
Parking Device for
Aircraft at
Reading, Penn
Airshow

Tysafe Device For Aircraft
1975

Hi's 60th birthday
with Mom, Mac Rubin & wife, Irv Feitel
Original Band Members in 1931

Hi and Marilyn
at a function
1979

At the 1999 Boston
AMICA Convention

Hi says "Bye!" till next year!

My chockstraps invention
with my airplane
1979

Tysafe 1974

Flying my cousin's
Airplane
2007

Flyin' Hy
and
My Plane

Joe Franklin TV show
1970

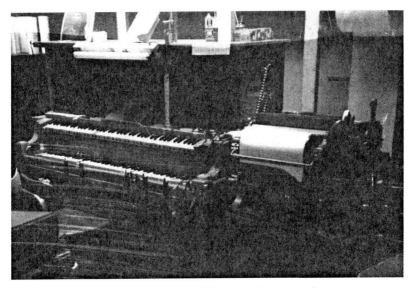

One of the piano roll recording machines
Could be Cook's piano at Aeolian

One of the pianos
used for making
piano rolls

At QRS, N. Bronx, NY 1964
Showing Stak-RAKS

Old and New way to keep piano rolls on piano
Use my Stak-Raks

Hi Babit at editing desk in
arranging room at QRS in Buffalo
1970

Using a CESSNA 150
to deliver piano rolls
1967

Hi Babit again sits at the QRS marking piano.

Hi Babit in the arranging room . . . what memories linger?

July 25, 1960
1st Solo flite
Initiation Throw in water.

All wet after
1st Solo
July 25, 1960

Hi and Hal Linden
2009

Hal Charm Orchestra at Polo Grounds 1953

Hi Babit on accordion, Hal Linden (movie star) on saxophone behind Hi

1950

**Daughter
Laurie Gail
1947-48**

Post-Headquarters at
Fort Leonard Wood
1944

Visiting Rube before he went to
England 1943

1939

Florrie on my
motorcycle 1940

Hi with
Glockenspiel

Feb. 16, 1941
One of the boys' accordion

Visiting an airfield near
Ft. McClellan 1941

Getting ready for Furlough trip
to New York 1941

1924

1931
At the
Bar Mitzvah

**Riding the wall at reservoir on Staten Island
1938**

**Hill climbing on motorcycle
1938**

1935
Graduate from
Erasmus Hall
High School

Mug shot
1930's?

Hi with parents
Esther and Max Babich
at La Guardia Airport going to Florida 1938

1935
Leader on Sax was Ben Walker
Hi on Accordion, Mac Rubin on Drums

**Ready to go to Atlanta
before collision
Aug 3, 1941**

My Motorcycle after the collision
Aug 3, 1941

1943
Parents' home

Florrie - Pregnant
At my Parent's house
1942

The O.W. Wuertz
Piano (1927)
On Furlough at Parents home—1943

On Furlough 1943
With Mom

Army - 1944
Scenes on desk is of wife Florrie
Both photos taken in Ozarks, MO

At the piano is Hi Babit with
Amparo Iturbi - sister of Jose Iturbi
Playing for the service personell

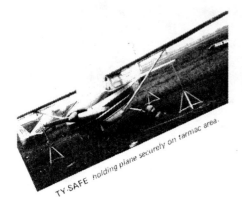
TY-SAFE *holding plane securely on tarmac area.*

TY-SAFE *maintains plane in negative nose down attitude.*

TY-SAFE *holding plane securely on grass area.*

Closeup showing TY-SAFE *use.*

Near Ft. McClellan - ALA
1941 - at an outing
of the JWB Group

**Hi and Florrie
at piano in parents home
1942, Brooklyn NY.**

At Fort Leonard Wood, MO
1943

Model Railroad layout of Trestle Invention in home, Brooklyn 1951

Exhibit A
Home - Brooklyn
Model RailRoad Layout of using
Trestles Invention

Visiting Rube at Camp Lee, VA
After escorting prisoner
to Atlantic City, NJ
Army Hospital

New Rolling Mill Produces Flat Wire for Western Industries

A new flat wire rolling mill, the only one of its kind on the west coast, has been placed in operation by Industrial Wire Products Corporation, 5649 Alhambra Avenue, Los Angeles 32, California.

The mill, which takes round wire and flattens it to sections from ⅜″ by ⅛″ thick to 3/16″ by 1/32″ thick, can produce flat wire in a variety of almost 500 different sizes. The flat wire can be furnished in coils, or if desired, cut into lengths to meet individual specifications.

According to E. R. Potter, president of the company, the

installation of the rolling mill marks another step in the company's aggressive program to supply western industry with its complete wire needs. "The need for flat wire is widespread in many industries today," Mr. Potter said. "Currently we are filling orders for toy and lamp manufacturers, as well as preparing to supply large quantities of flat wire to the aircraft industry.

"The rolling mill can handle all types of wire, including Brite Basic, Annealed, Copper, Brass and other alloys. It has an operational capacity of approximately 2000 pounds per day," Mr. Potter continued, "thereby enabling us to make prompt delivery of the flat wire to industrial users quickly and efficiently."

MAKING SALES WITHOUT SAMPLES

SOMETHING old but something new in the field of merchandising has been introduced to manufacturers and their representatives to increase sales, and at the same time ease the burden on the salesman.

This new compact and portable, almost pocket-sized gimmick will bring the complete line of the salesman or manufacturer before the customer in full color and in life-like dimensions.

The idea was developed by a commercial photographer in New York, Herman Babich, who uses the name of "*Stereo by Hy*."

Stereo — short for stereopticons or three-dimensional pictures — is the new life-like, true perspective method of presenting a complete line.

Use Both Eyes

The term "stereo" has been loosely used by many of the photographers selling their service to the manufacturers. There is only one way to view stereo pictures — you have to use both eyes to look at two almost identical prints or transparencies through optical lenses. When viewed in this manner, the two pictures become one, and a feeling of depth and perspective is apparent. To test for depth and perspective, hold the viewer and look first with one eye and then the other, and then open both eyes. It is said you can almost reach out and hold the object. It has realism!

Mr. Babich has developed a new package that also consists of a viewer, and it is low-priced. It uses a reel that contains, not one set of pictures, but seven sets of pictures. These are viewed in sequence by the mere flipping of a lever. A light attachment that uses either batteries or plug-in transformer can be attached or detached at will. The viewer can be used without this light attachment by just facing any strong light.

Shows Toy In Actual Use

The advantages are apparent. The retailer can see seven different types of toys or games by just flipping the lever. He doesn't have to stand and feed a new slide in for each new view. The retailer can also use this viewer to illustrate and explain how a toy or game is to be operated or played.

The pictures can show youngsters playing or using the game or toy. No matter how much explaining or instructing the retailer or salesman will do, the stereo pictures will do it more quickly and simply.

The slide container holding up to seven reels or forty-nine views measures only four inches square by one-quarter inch thick. The viewer with the light attachment measures only four by six inches. The whole unit can fit into any small brief case. The salesman need not carry around a multitude of bulky samples.

Certain action toys or games can be graphically illustrated in sequence on these reels. Trains, wheel toys, dolls, all seem to come alive on these reels.

The comments by those who have seen these stereo pictures have ranged from terrific, ooh and ah, to sensational. This is a must for promoting and stimulating more sales.

♦

• Because it is pleased with the production picture, the government will endeavor to dispose of its synthetic rubber plants to private firms. Washington sees the outlook for synthetic as vastly improved, and that consumption will remain high. Price of natural rubber, after several weeks of remaining around 28½ cents a pound, has dropped again.

Hi Babit trio
at Balalaika Restaurant
1957-1967
Hi Babit - piano, Vinnie Cammizi - drums,
Morty Ross - Sax-Clar-Violin

Figure 8 Over-and-Under
AMERICAN FLYER TRAIN SYSTEM

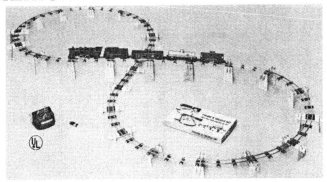

- 260" of 2-RAIL TRACK
- LOCOMOTIVE HAS PULL-MOR POWER...CAN HAUL OVER 40 CARS!
- REVERSIBLE
- WORM-GEAR DRIVE
- AUTHENTIC SCALE MODEL!

1958 ADVERTISING TRAIN No. 20123

Pieces	Description	List Price	Pieces	Description	List Price
1	"Atlantic" Loco and Tender with Pull-Mor	$19.00	6	Straight Track @ .30	1.80
1	Gondola	4.50	1	Track Terminal	.25
1	Tank	5.50	1	40-Watt Transformer, UL & CSA Approved	6.95
1	Caboose	4.95	26	Piece Trestle Set	4.95
20	Curve Track @ .30	6.00	1	Instruction Sheet	
			59 Pieces — Total if Purchased Separately		$53.90

D2052

Babit Industries Inc. PRE-FLIGHT with LINE-O-SITE — *BEFORE* you start your trip.

LINE-O-SITE
A 3 DIMENSIONAL NAVIG-AID

PILOT (name & home base)_____

DATE_____

CLOSE FLIGHT PLAN UPON ARRIVAL

FLIGHT PLAN

FLIGHT LOG

REMEMBER! It is the RESPONSIBILITY of the pilot to KNOW – HIS – AND – the PLANE's LIMITATIONS!

FUEL – on board gals/lbs – G P H			Fuel Tank Switching Tach &/or Hour		POSITION REPORTING					
					ACFT & #	POSITION	ALT	VFR/IFR	FROM/TO	NEXT FIX
					Winds aloft:			Pireps:		

AIRPORTS – Elev & Alt. Setting   RUNWAYS – wind/dens.alt.etc   RADIO FREQS

DEPARTING
ATIS_____ VOR_____
GRND_____ RB_____
CL.DEL_____ ILS_____
TWR_____ LOM_____
T/O TIME   TXDR_____

DESTINATION
ATIS_____ VOR_____
APC_____ RB_____
TXDR_____ ILS_____
TWR_____ LOM_____
LDG TIME   GRND_____

ALTERNATE
ATIS_____ VOR_____
APC_____ RB_____
TXDR_____ ILS_____
TWR_____ LOM_____
GRND_____

CHECKPOINTS	HDG	DISTANCES		FLIGHT TIMING		SPEEDS		RADIO AIDS – for Routes & X-Checking		
		POINT/TOTAL	EST / ACT / TOTAL		HOUR/TACH	TAS / GS		NAV 1 – Freq/Radial	NAV 2 – Freq/Radial	ADF

TC	WIND MPH FROM	WCA R+ L–	TH	VAR W+ E–	MH	DEV	CH	WEATHER ADVISORIES

TYPE FLITE PLAN VFR	IFR	DVFR	FROM	TO (Arpt & City)	ACFT TYPE & EQUIP	ACFT IDENT	PEOPLE

ROUTE OF FLITE   MILEAGE   COLOR

TRUE AIRSPEED KTS	EST TIME ENROUTE HR MIN	FUEL ON BOARD HR MIN	GPH	RANGE	FUEL REQ'D	EST T/O TIME	CRUISING ALT

WEIGHTS   GROSS   USEFUL ALLOW. LOAD: GAS   PEOPLE   BAGS

SPECIAL EQUIPMENT SUFFIX
X =Transponder, no code
T =Transponder, with 64 code capability
U =Transponder, with 4096 code capability
D =DME
L =DME and transponder, no code

B =DME and transponder, with 64 code capability
A =DME and transponder, with 4096 code capability
F =No code transponder and approved area navigation
C =4096 code transponder and approved area navigation
S =64 code transponder and approved area navigation
W =No transponder and approved area navigation

➤ **CLOSE FLIGHT PLAN**
TIE-DOWN WITH **TY-SAFE**

AERO-SAF-T-PRODUCTS

HI BABIT - - GEN. MGR.
718-317-1005 ---- 201-939-8888
94 EAST MACON AVE. STATEN ISLAND, N.Y. 10308

 # AERO-SAF-T-PRODUCTS

PLANE SAF-T IS OUR BUSINESS

Another piano roll making set-up could be in J. Lawrence Cook's room at Aeolian Hall

Entertaining Music

Hi BABiT

at the Organ

Trio

JU 2-2800
IN 9-8984
IN 9-7644

152 CLARKSON AVENUE
BROOKLYN 26, N. Y.

Wedding Reception
Sept. 21, 1963

```
WEDDINGS
   BAR
 MITZVAHS
   ETC.
  IN OUR
 MEDALLION
   AND
   MURAL
   ROOMS
```

Margueritta and Fred
Ontmuller

The *Balalaika*

RESTAURANT

645 Bronx River Road
Yonkers, New York
BE 7-0685 - 9822

Donaghy

Sing - A - Long

For Your Dining Pleasure
-- Presents --

Music Nitely

HI BABIT

entertaining you with

The "NEW" Exciting Sounds of the

X T P HAMMOND ORGAN

AND

The "OLD" Nostalgic Sounds of the

PLAYER PIANO

Donaghy Steak House

KI 8-3377
KI 6-9571

5523 Broadway, Bronx, N. Y.

Ample Parking

WHAT'S YOUR FAVORITE SELECTION?

COME SAY HELLO — OR GIVE TO WAITER

1. ....

2. ....

3. ....

4. ....

Hi Babit played a party for
Gene Krupa
Drummer for Benny Goodman
1965

1970
at Donaghy's Steak House
Bronx, NY

My Line-O-Site Invention for Navigation Learning and using

Line-O-Site invention
1974

USE THIS CONVENIENT ORDER BLANK:

From: HI WIRE INDUSTRIAL COMPANY
781 EAST 136th ST.
Bronx, New York 10454

Ship To:

NAME _____
ADDRESS _____
CITY _____
STATE _____ ZIP ____

Bill To:

NAME _____
ADDRESS _____
CITY _____
STATE _____ ZIP ____
SEND ADDITIONAL FOLDERS _____
DATE _____ SIGNED _____

Additional Folders Sent on Request
for Mailing to Dealer's Customers.

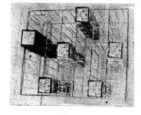

THE PIANO ROLL
STAK-RAKS
Designed by Hi Babit
QRS Music Arranger

IDEAL FOR HOMES AND DEALERS
PERFECT FOR QUICK REFERENCE
NO HUNTING - HOME DECOR STYLED
BRASS PLATED - MAXIMUM STORAGE

Large
Economy
Model
Holds
Triple
Storage
For Less
Than Double
The Price.

83 ROLLS
LIST PRICE
31.50
Model No.
875

Holds
29 Rolls
"PORTABLE"

Model No.
425
LIST PRICE
15.95

THE
OLD
AND
THE
NEW

THE
NEW
MUSIC
STAN-RAKS
PAT. PEND.

It's A Music Stand!
It's A Music Cabinet!
IT'S NEAT!

VISIT US AT THE
CONRAD HILTON - ROOM 760
IN CHICAGO, JULY 10-14

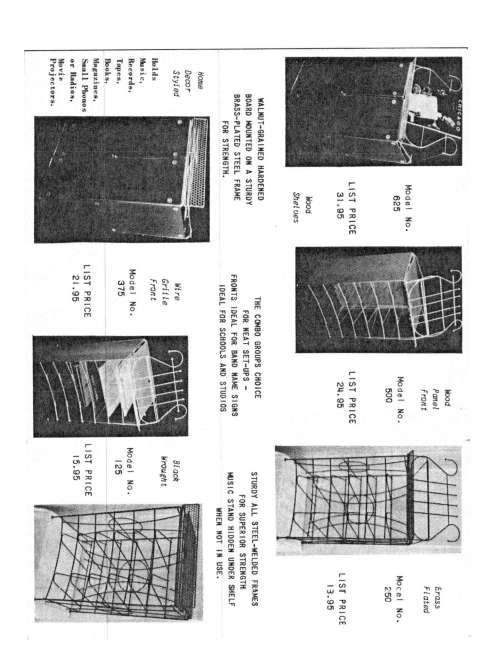

Model No. 625
LIST PRICE 31.95

Wood Shelves

Model No. 500
LIST PRICE 24.95

Wood Panel Front

Model No. 250
LIST PRICE 13.95

Brass Plated

STURDY ALL STEEL-WELDED FRAMES
FOR SUPERIOR STRENGTH
MUSIC STAND HIDDEN UNDER SHELF
WHEN NOT IN USE.

THE COMBO GROUPS CHOICE
FOR NEAT SET-UPS -
FRONTS IDEAL FOR BAND NAME SIGNS
IDEAL FOR SCHOOLS AND STUDIOS

WALNUT-GRAINED HARDENED
BOARD MOUNTED ON A STURDY
BRASS-PLATED STEEL FRAME
FOR STRENGTH.

Home
Decor
Styled

Holds
Music,
Records,
Tapes,
Books,
Magazines,
Small Phonos
or Radios,
Movie
Projectors.

Model No. 375
LIST PRICE 21.95

Wire Grille Front

Model No. 125
LIST PRICE 15.95

Black Wrought

1975
At Donaghy's
restaurant
Bronx, NY

Playing on the
Joe Franklin TV show
1975

From the Herald, January 10, 1999 — Sent in by Roland Chisnell and Keith Bigger

AMICA People

'AFTER I TUNE, I PLAY': Hi Babit tries out 88 Cafe Society's piano after tuning. 'I've gotten a lot of parties that way,' he says.

Human touch

Seasoned piano tuner's talent is all about playing it by ear

By DANIEL DEVISE, Herald Staff Writer

Hi Babit, 81, tunes pianos aided only by his ears, a wrench and a small steel fork. His pitch isn't perfect. But it is good enough.

Piano tuning is an art, and sound is an imperfect science. Traditional Piano tuners such as Babit eschew electronics. A properly tuned piano, they believe, can only be the work of human hands and human ears.

"I don't have perfect pitch." Babit said. "I'd be crazy if I had perfect pitch. I have relative pitch. Sometimes, relatives are better."

Babit, who lives in Coconut Creek, has tuned pianos by ear for most of his adult life. He is also an accomplished pianist with large hands that can span 11 white keys, or about an octave and a half. For three decades, he made a living by punching rolls for player pianos.

The man born Herman Babich is also an inventor and a licensed pilot. He made regular flights back to his home state of New York to tune pianos until the rising costs of flying his own airplane became prohibitive. Acoustic pianos aren't such common sights in American homes as they once were. But business

IN TUNE: Hi Babit, 81, tightens piano strings to the right pitch. A traditional piano tuner, he eschews electronics.

is brisk at Bobb's Pianos and organs, a local chain that hires Babit to tune pianos, and at such restaurants as 88 Café Society in Hollywood, where heavy use requires Babit to tune the Kawai grand piano twice a month.

"I can knock a piano out of tune in a couple of hours when I'm playing," he said. "I'm a heavy player."

Variations in humidity can also change the pitch of a piano string by causing the soundboard to expand or contract. The piano industry recommends tunings at least twice a year for older pianos, three or four times a year for new ones. Babit charges $65 for a tuning.

His day begins when he strikes an A-440 - concert A - on his tuning fork. He holds it to the harp-shaped metal soundboard to produce a loud hum. Then, he goes to work.

Each piano key moves a hammer that strikes three separate strings. Babit uses tiny wedges to silence two strings at a time as he tunes the third. He tightens or loosens the string by turning a modified socket wrench. He tests one pitch against another, listening to layers of harmonics. As the notes slide into tune, Babit listens for a faint harmonic pulse that slows and eventually stops.

"There's a certain lilt or wave that I look for," he said. "It's hard to explain."

Modern electronic meters can be used in place of the trusty tuning fork, but Babit doesn't put much stock in them.

An electronic tuning meter typically will produce a piano with an upper register that is slightly sharp. Tuners who work by ear subtly flatten or sharpen certain notes to place the entire piano in tune.

"If they're a good tuner, they don't use the meter," said Mark Messingschlager of Bobb's Pianos and Organs, who sometimes hires Babit to fine-tune pianos already tuned by others. "Anybody can be a tuner if all you have to do is look at the meter. That means you're no good."

Babit starts at a piano's center and works his way up to the highest notes. Then, he works his way down to the low register.

"Boy, the top went out more than I thought," he said, tickling the ivories of the piano at 88 Café Society on a recent morning. "Hear how out of tune that is?"

Young Herman Babich worked in a factory where his father tailored women's clothes. As a high school student, he worked for his father in the afternoons and played piano in dance clubs at night.

As an adult, Herman shortened his name for show business purposes and proceeded to popularize it in the restaurants of Yonkers.

In 1963, he went to work for a player-piano company in the South Bronx, playing notes into a punch-press machine that spat out music rolls. Over the next 30 years, his signature went on dozens of rolls ranging from Beer Barrel Polka and Chopsticks to Suspicious Minds and Muskrat Love.

Babit stopped making player piano rolls in the early 1980s but remains a celebrity among aficionados of mechanical player pianos.

The Babits, Hi and Marilyn, moved to Florida in 1993. He still plays parties and clubs for $75 an hour.

Sometimes, he gets gigs on the strength of the improvisational chords he bangs out on a piano when he's done with a tuning.

"I've gotten a lot of parties that way," he said. "Because after I tune, I play."

For more information, call Hi Babit at 954-984-0033.

TICKLING THE IVORIES: Hi Babit started playing piano in clubs as a teenager; he still plays parties.

TRIBUTE TO HI BABIT ON HIS 90TH BIRTHDAY

(By Stuart Addison)

HI BABIT'S THE GUY WE'RE HERE TO TOAST
THE CHAP WHO REALLY DESERVES TO BOAST
BECAUSE HE REALLY KNOWS THE MOST
ABOUT MUSICAL STUFF FROM COAST TO COAST

HE TUNES AND HE FIXES ALL PIANOS AND PLAYS
HIS FINGERS ARE SKILLED, AND THEY KNOW ALL THE WAYS
TO MAKE MUSIC MAGIC, TO THRILL AND AMAZE
AND LIFT UP OUR SPIRITS AND BRIGHTEN OUR DAYS

WHEN DANCERS COMPLAIN THAT THE MUSIC'S TOO SLOW
THIS MUSICAL GURU KNOWS WHICH WAY TO GO
AND A SONG THAT'S TOO LOW IF IT'S WRITTEN IN B
HI MOVES IN A FLASH, AND IT'S NOW SUNG IN C

WE NEED HIM, WE LOVE HIM, EACH ONE IS HIS FAN
WITHOUT HIM WE'D JUST HAVE A MUSICAL PLAN
BUT HI BRINGS IT LIFE JUST AS ONLY HI CAN
THIS KING OF THE KEYBOARD, OUR GREAT PIANO MAN!!!

HAPPY 90TH BIRTHDAY, HI, OUR SUPERMAN OF THE 88 KEYS!!!

BOBB'S Pianos & Organs

PRODUCTS OF BABIT INDUSTRIES

<u>TY-SAFE</u> - - - - - A PARKING DEVICE FOR AIRCRAFT

<u>LINE-O-SITE</u> - - - A TRAVEL DEVICE FOR AIRCRAFT

<u>Q*U*A*D*S</u> - - - - A FOUR HAND CHECKER GAME (FOUR PLAYERS)

<u>BABY CARRIAGE</u> with AUTOMATIC BRAKING when HAND RELEASED

<u>CONSTANT TEACHER</u> - MUSIC LESSONS with TAPE & BOOKS

<u>PERFECT ACCOMPANIST</u> - - PIANO ROLLS with ONE PART WITHHELD
FOR ACCOMPANIMENT

<u>MUSIC BOOKS</u> with EDGE-ANIMATED FLIP PIX (MOVIE STYLE)

<u>FOLDING CHAIRS</u> with FOLD-OUT MUSIC STANDS FOR ORCHESTRAS

<u>PIANO ACTIONS</u> with CASSETTE TYPE INDIVIDUAL IN/OUT PARTS

<u>SONG TITLES</u>

I LOVE YOU, I WANT YOU	NO BUT YOU
AWAY FROM YOU	WHEN ONCE WE WERE IN LOVE
IN LOVE WITH A DREAM	JAZZ WALTZ
THIS I'D LIKE TO KNOW	HOW ABOUT THAT
TEARS OF MY LOVE	STRAUS STYLE WALTZ
FIRST LETS DO THE CHA CHA CHA	FRENCH STYLE WALTZ
MOON ABOVE US	BLUES STYLE WALTZ
DEAR MR. SANTA CLAUS	
IT MAKES NO NEVER MIND	
I'LL KEEP WALKIN'	
RAG-A-MA-ZAG	

1586 E. Commercial Blvd., Ft. Lauderdale   Florida 33334 • Broward 776-1221

Four Babich Kids (July 2006)

**Hi Babit
Checking roll for a CD with
Danny Geoghegan who
invented the device
to make my CD's
2007**

At Polan's house
Melville L.I. WY.
2007 AMICA Meeting

The Babich Siblings
2010

Chapter 5

The Piano-Roll Years

*N*ow we come to the era that made me famous? So here's the story of how I got into the piano roll business. I had seen a New York *Daily News* story of the Imperial Industries company in the Bronx, New York. I think it was the Sunday center section around Christmas time of 1962. I figured that someday I would go up there to see how they made piano rolls. Being an inventor of sorts, I wanted to make a toy player piano for my students to teach them more about rhythm and music.

One day in late June of 1963 I saw an ad in the *New York Times* for a Pianist-Arranger wanted at the Imperial Industries, Bronx, New York. I did remember the company name and figured that here's my chance to see how they make piano rolls. I answered the ad and made an appointment to visit the factory. In those days I was still playing at the Balalaika restaurant in Yonkers, New York, and teaching and tuning pianos.

The Flying Piano Roll Man

I went to the factory, which was located in the South Bronx at 136th Street and Willow Avenue and met Herman Kortlander. Herman was then the manager of the Imperial Industries, while Mrs. Kortlander, the widow of Max Kortlander, stayed in the office. Herman took me to the arranging room where I met Dick Watson. It was a small room with only an old upright piano and a punch press machine next to it. The piano was open—no front board—and had a ruler-like device on the front of it in an upright position, with a claw device attached to it. On the floor under the keyboard was a treadle to activate the punch press machine.

Dick Watson started to explain how they made the piano rolls. He said you don't play the piano. You hold down certain notes of your arrangement and activate the punch press machine via the treadle bar on the floor below the keyboard. You can do one punch at a time, or hold your foot on the treadle to activate the punch press machine for a series of holes in the first paper master. He said that they used twelve punches for a quarter note, or one beat because it was a good dividing number for the different valued notes. A one-eighth note got six punches; a triplet, four punches; and a one-sixteenth note, three punches. So it was a good dividing number. I laughed about it because I was thinking of flying the military airplanes by the numbers, and now I see that you made music the same way by the numbers. So it's all a math game. I used that math game to make my piano roll arrangement stylings. I'll explain later.

The ruler in front of the piano was marked off in twelve-line increments. A claw movement in front of the ruler went up one step every time the punch press machine moved. That way you could keep count of where you were. Also since music is repeated phrases, all you had to do was to make certain sections of a song, and then with the master copy machine, make a complete piano roll according to the arranger's notes of which sections to copy and in what order.

Because I started to make different style arrangements, I made and used different marked rulers according to the amount of punches I gave to one beat. I sometimes used an eighteen-count punch for one beat, or a sixteen- or twenty-count. It varied with the kind of song I was doing. For slow ballads I would use the longer numbered counts. For editing purposes I made a series of multiple punched templates that were marke with the counted lines to quickly check the position of the notes for octaves or tenths, etc. I used those templates to either cut in another note or to delete a note. I designed templates for easy editing. They told me where each note was on the master. It made life easy!

I'll try to explain about repeated phrases. Most of the songs that were written years ago were what we usually call the A-B-A form. Most of the songs of that era were made up of thirty-two measures, or thirty-two bars. Bars and measures mean the same thing. The first eight measures of the song was the "A," and the second part was also the "A," because it was a repeat of the first "A." The middle part of the song was the "B," and usually the last eight bars was the same as the first eight, so it was the "A" again. Once you made the A and B sections, you could, after editing those sections, give both sections to the copy master machine worker to make the final master for the production process.

I want to explain about the editing process. I had a desk or table that had a raised section with a spindle on it to hold the master roll. The desk was not flat but had a forty to forty-five degree sloped platform on which you rolled down the master, and you could examine the punches or the holes with the templates to verify the position of the notes from bass to treble. I would draw a line across the master and give it an alphabet letter. I would mark another line at the end of the master with another letter. That way, the master machine worker just had to follow the lettered sections; and you could, in a few hours, come out with a piano roll.

Because of that system, if they had three choruses on the roll, they were usually the same arrangement of that chorus. It was a quick way to get a piano roll finished. I'm sure that if you were to listen to the older piano rolls, should I say, before my time, you will hear the same three arrangements of that song. I did the same thing in my first three or four piano rolls. I did it the way I was told to. I was told to listen to a record and try to make the roll like the record. There were also a sixteen-and-sixteen bar style of songs with just a slight change for the ending.

For the editing, I had a small hole puncher, like a leather-craft hole-punching tool, to punch in holes that I needed if I wanted to add any notes. Also I had rolls of one-quarter-inch-wide scotch tape to cover holes or notes that I didn't want on the master. I assume that type of narrow Scotch tape had to be special-ordered. That was not an ordinary sized roll of tape you could buy in a store. To cut in notes that I wanted to add, I had an X-Acto knife. Those were the editing tools.

I also had a big ruler with the letter names of the piano keys that you could use on the master to check if your arrangement had the right notes in the right place. I gave that ruler to someone at AMICA for their collection.

Kortlander asked me to play something on the piano, and figuring that most of the piano rolls had a honky-tonk sound, I played some of that style music. Kortlander asked me if I would consider making piano rolls for them. I thought quickly about it and decided to do it. It seems that Dick Watson worked from 9:00 a.m. to 1:00 p.m., and they were looking for someone to work from 1:00 p.m. to 5:00 p.m. Since I didn't have to fight traffic in the early morning, and I lived in Brooklyn, and since the Bronx was halfway to my job at the Balalaika restaurant in Yonkers, and I was tuning pianos all over New York, I said OK and started to work there.

They gave me a salary of $125.00 a week. The first roll they had me do was "This Is All I Ask." They gave me a record of Tony Bennett singing it and told me to make it like the record. Even when Ramsi Tick bought the company and moved it to Buffalo, New York, he had the same idea of do it like the record. They didn't realize that there were a lot of bombastic sounds on some of the records and that if you made those same sounds on the roll, it would be hard to hear the melody. Most of the bombastic sounds were in the bass where the sound is heavy, and this would overshadow the light sounds of the treble melody lines.

I know this for a fact, because when I'd tune a player piano and the customer had a roll with those sounds, I always had complaints that they didn't enjoy the piano roll. I have to add they were usually not my rolls. I tried to explain those complaints to the bosses, but deaf ears. I had other ideas of how a piano roll should be made to sound better and more enjoyable for listening. I wanted to make a roll that sounded as though a live person was playing it. I tried to get away from the mechanical sound of a piano roll.

I recently heard a piano roll on YouTube on the Internet that did what I said previously. The roll had a full bass section for the accompaniment but only had a single melody line. The melody line was lost and hard to hear because the bass came across loud. It was an old piano roll that was probably from the 1930s or the '40s.

I have recently been making CDs of my piano rolls. I have a big collection of audio tapes of the rolls that I made. When I made tapes of my rolls, I was not thinking that someday I would make CDs of them. It was just a way to hear some of my finished rolls and to have a record of them. When I found and heard a tape of the recording of my first piano roll, "This Is All I Ask," I was very surprised that it sounded as good as it did for my first attempt. I am and always will be critical of my rolls. Every time I listen to my tapes, I think that I could have made a better arrangement of that roll. It's not that I'm a fusspot, but when I play live, I'm always looking for a better way to play that song. So I'm my worst critic.

Even now when I'm rehearsing a show, I never know what kind of background I'm going to give the singers or the dancers. Each rehearsal has a different background. This is a habit I got into because I'm usually looking at and following the singers or dancers;

I know that at times they are apt to goof, and since the written music would not do me any good, I developed the habit of rehearsing without the manuscript. After a lot of rehearsing, the arrangements are in my head. A singer may goof by inadvertently skipping a section of the music, or the dancers may goof by forgetting which steps they had to do. They say that's what rehearsals are for. I always caution a singer or dancer at showtime that if they should goof, just keep performing, and I will follow and cover them.

Now to get back to the piano-roll making. While Dick Watson and I were the only roll makers in the Bronx, I had heard of J. Lawrence Cook but had never met him. I was told that he worked for Aeolian. On the final copy master machine was Rudy Martin. He just worked the final master machine. I made it my business to learn how to run the master machine because I sometimes worked late after the other workers left for the day. I was able to immediately run off my new arrangements and listen to them so that I could make corrections if I didn't like the way it sounded or move on to the next part of the arrangement. Sometimes Dick Watson would ask me to run off his first masters, and if Rudy wasn't there, I would run his masters and make a copy for him to listen to.

After about the fourth or fifth roll, I decided to make some changes in the way I made piano rolls. Since I get bored with the sameness of the sounds of arrangements, I decided to make rolls with two or three different arrangements on them. I don't remember which roll I started making those changes on, but about three or four months after I began making the newer styled piano rolls, Mrs. Kortlander called me in to her office. I asked if I did something wrong, and she said no, that she only wanted to tell me that most of the customers were asking only for the Hi Babit piano rolls. I then realized that people do listen to arrangements and appreciate different styles.

Of course I felt good about it, and it boosted my ego. I wanted to make piano rolls that sounded as if a live piano player was performing. I didn't want the roll to sound honky-tonk. I began to make my arrangements to include tempo changes typical of a professional pianist, even though the piano roll was running at a constant speed. It was a simple trick, and it seemed to make my rolls sound better. That trick, as I call it, was to merely work with the math of the notes. All I did was to either add or subtract punches to get the effect I wanted. Douglas Henderson from Maine thinks that I changed the format of piano-roll making. I want to thank him for that observation and statement. He said that other older arrangers before me made arrangements according to a formula, but I didn't.

In those days, going into customers' homes and seeing the piano rolls stacked on top of the piano, I invented or designed a rack to hold those boxes of piano rolls. When you pulled a piano roll box from the stacked group of rolls on top of the piano, the boxes would usually tumble, and that led me to this new invention, which would facilitate easy selection by using pigeonholes in a wire unit. I made my first prototype using balsa wood (since I used balsa wood in my airplane models). I designed the rack to individually hold the boxes so that you could take one box out and put it back in the same place. I called the device Stak-Rak. I had two models: one to hold twenty-nine rolls and one to hold eighty-three rolls. I'll explain the odd numbers. Five regular roll boxes equaled the width of four large medley-roll boxes, so I had a small rack of 25 + 4 = 29, and the large rack held 75 + 8 = 83. I thought that those two sizes were enough.

The reason behind the stacking idea came from the design. There were two folding handles on the small rack for carrying purposes which, when opened, became the slot for inserting the legs of the Stak-Rak. You could put one on top of the other and get it as high as you wanted to. The legs would lock the two Stak-Raks together because of the folding-handles device design.

I showed it to Mrs. Kortlander, but she said she was not interested in getting into making those racks. I went to a wire company in the Bronx and had them make me the two sizes. I called myself Hi-Wire Industrial Company. I made the designs for the flyers, and each flyer went out with every piano roll shipped from the factory. I also went around to all the piano-roll stores in the northeast and found that I could sell. I had never considered myself a salesman. I did have a foot in the door advantage when I went to those music stores; all I had to say was just, "I'm Hi Babit from the QRS factory," and I had an eager audience and was able to sell my Stak-Raks quickly and easily.

I always avoided selling because of my stuttering. I found that I could overcome that stuttering from necessity. I used to explain that a lot of my accomplishments were made because of that word "necessity." If you want to stay in any certain business, you had better learn from necessity what to do to accomplish it. My ear training came from playing for singers, and I laughingly say, from playing Jewish weddings. The cantors all thought they were opera stars. They would tell me that they will do the Blessings in the key of A, but they would invariably change to different keys like going to B flat or A flat or the key of G, and if I didn't go and change keys with them, they would question if I know how to play. Again I say, "That's why I do most of my shows without the written music because if the entertainer goofs, I just follow them, and they later thank me for covering them." When I first started with the bands in 1931, I couldn't do what I'm able to do now. So from NECESSITY I learned and developed capabilities.

My flyers for the Stak-Raks went out enclosed in every piano-roll box that was sold or shipped, until Ramsi Tick bought the company, and he cut it out. Ramsi came out with just a plain cabinet with shelves and put it in his catalog. It was not the same as mine! At the Namm show in Chicago in 1964, I used the QRS room at the show to show my Stak-Raks. What impressed me and built up my ego was that on every floor at the Conrad Hilton where the show was held, all you heard on every floor that had player pianos was my piano roll of "Granada" being played. That roll seemed to show off the capabilities of a player piano. Again I was very flattered by their selection of my piano roll.

While in the Bronx, I invited Herman Kortlander to come to the Balalaika restaurant and hear my group play. This was just before we changed from a supper club to a catering place. He heard me play the song "Dancing in the Dark." He liked my arrangement and asked me to make a piano roll of it. I did. It is QRS roll no. 5181. I'm sorry that I didn't include the verse to that song on the roll because when I play it live at parties or shows, I always include the verse and the chorus. If I had to do that roll again, I would start with the chorus then go back to the verse, and then repeat the chorus with a big ending. Now when I listen to my old arrangements, I think I shoulda, woulda, coulda done better.

Visitors would sometimes come to make a tour of the factory. One day a woman came to tour and mentioned that she was from Isreal. I had just finished making the roll of Hava Nagilah (QRS 9943) and played it for her. She was delighted with my arrangement and said that there was nothing like it in Isreal, and that she would take back a few rolls to show them there and give out as presents. It's on one of my CD's.

When Ramsi Tick bought the company and decided to move them up to Buffalo, New York, he asked me and Dick Watson if we would also move. He got most of the workers to move, but Dick and I declined. Rudy martin told me that he was going to move to Buffalo and start making piano rolls there. The day they moved the factory, Dick and I were there to get our things. Rudy asked me if I would show him some of the tricks I used in making the piano rolls, and I said yes. Dick Watson said, "Are you crazy to give him your ideas?" I told Dick that the tricks I was showing Rudy were only mechanical tricks but that he would never think like me about how to make an arrangement.

After Imperial Industries moved and I went to Aeolian to make rolls for them, Rudy would ask me to bring my new ones when I went to Buffalo to work for QRS. He wanted to peruse them and see what I did. I think I've said it before. Everyone has their own styling, whether it be writing arrangements of just playing piano or piano-roll arranging. Cook, Watson, Martin and I had our own style.

After Imperial Industries moved to Buffalo, Ramsi officially changed the name to QRS Music Rolls Inc. Mr. Furlong from Aeolian called and asked me to make piano rolls for them. At first they put me in their factory at 146th Street in the South Bronx near where the old Imperial Company was. That was the factory where they made all their pianos, including the player pianos. They were just a couple of blocks off the Bruckner Expressway, and they had a neon lighted piano on top of the building which you could see if you were driving South on the Bruckner Expressway.

They had a new machine there to make rolls, which was interesting, but after a few attempts to make a piano roll with that machine, I turned it down. Why? The concept was good. It was a machine that if you played very slowly could make a piano roll of your playing. Instead of a paper master, they used a Mylar plastic sheet. It's almost impossible to see the holes in that master for editing. I had to invent an editing machine to use with that Mylar master. Another reason for not liking that machine was that it was made for only two hands. Most of my piano rolls were three- and four-hand arrangements. I preferred making my big arrangements like I did at Imperial Industries.

I was on the sixth floor in the Bronx factory. There was a worker who worked on the transmissions for the player piano. One day I asked him a simple question. I told him that I tuned pianos and that I had complaints about the transmission units in the newer ones. I told him that earlier models didn't have problems, but the later ones did. His answer was, "If I don't make changes, I won't have a job." That ploy happens in almost every business.

Some businesses like to stay with the same way of doing things, like in my father's shop. I had to spread out material that we used for linings in coats or the heavier wool coat material and get it ready for cutting. They had a new machine that could automatically spread the material on the large tables. I asked my father that if he got that machine, it would speed up cutting and getting the bundles ready for the sewing machine operators. He said, "No, we will do it the way we always did it." So much for progress!

My earlier computer programs were easy to work with, and the later "improved"? versions were impossible to use. I'm sure that if you are computer savvy, you know what I mean. I think the same goes for automobiles and for most businesses. Make changes and sell the new programs with the new problems. Ha-ha-ha!

After a couple of months of struggling with the Bronx machine, the company asked me to work with Cook in the Fifty-seventh Street building. That's when I first met J. Lawrence Cook. He worked on the sixth floor of the Fifty-seventh Street building in Manhattan, and he worked there from nine to five. Aeolian gave me a key to the building so that I could come there, park my car in front at 6:00 p.m., and work there at night. For me it was great because I was alone in that building, and I could come and go as I please. I was used to working at night because of my band work. I was also able to check some of the Sheraton chain of hotels that I was servicing for piano tuning. I found it much easier to work at night because it was easier to park, and most of the rooms where I had to tune were vacant.

Herman Kortlander also went to work for Aeolian as a manager for song selections. However, I usually had carte blanche in picking what I wanted to do. I had no trouble with Cook or Kortlander, who liked a lot of my selections, unlike QRS where they told me what titles I had to make. Some of the numbers that QRS picked I didn't think were good numbers; at Aeolian I could pick what I thought would make a good piano roll. At QRS, Ramsi was of the opinion that if a record sold a million copies, QRS should have a piano roll of that song. Some of those records were too bombastic, or they didn't have what I thought was a good melodic line.

For instance, in Peggy Lee's rendition of "Is That All There Is?" she really doesn't sing but talks most of it by telling a story and only sings about eight bars. On the insistence of Ramsi, I made that roll, but I think that it's more like a solo piano selection. It's not a singable song. There were many songs I turned down for Ramsi. I remember that I once made a list of things to do with rolls, like certain types of medleys, or certain types of selections. I thought I lost that list until one day I was in Ramsi's office and found it on his desk. When I questioned him about it, his answer was, "You're not here all the time, and I can use it." I think that a lot of my ideas were used by Ramsi, but he never credited me for them.

I started the *Play-A-Long* series and had visions of lots of titles, but they only let me make two. First I did "Down at Papa Joe's" and then "Chopsticks". Ramsi asked if I could write words for "Chopsticks" since they liked words on the piano roll. I composed seven stanzas of words for "Chopsticks" and thought maybe some kiddy shows would pick it up, but it never happened. There were letters to QRS for more *Play-A-Long*, and years later they came out with "Heart and Soul." I didn't make that one but I think it has my name on it.

I'd like to talk about one of my experiments with long playing or medley rolls. Most medley rolls run about seven to eight minutes. Well, I decided to experiment and make a long-playing roll on the small-sized two-inch roll. I chose a classical piece, which would be a good example and a challenge to do. I chose Georges Enesco's Roumanian Rhapsody No.1. If you can find it, it is QRS 10-000. It runs for about seven to eight minutes. I put it on my CD No. 4. I think it does sound almost as good as a duo-art or Ampico roll. You be the judge.

I used a shorter count to get the desired results. The paper runs at a constant speed, but the music sound varies from slow to fast runs and melody lines. As I mentioned before, it's all math! I still can't figure why, with hundreds of arrangers before me, no one thought of the same things to do that I could do. One problem, if you want to call it a problem, was that in order to play that long-playing number, you had to have a player piano that could play at a slow speed of forty or fifty. A lot of those older big uprights, I found, couldn't play that slowly.

When working for Aeolian, I wanted to try some new ideas that I thought would help sell more player pianos. I designed a program called "The Constant Teacher" to help in teaching music. I also had an idea for an accompanying roll, which was based on Music Minus One where I would make a roll to accompany glee clubs or little trios or quartets when they couldn't get a good pianist to accompany them. I called it "The Perfect Accompanist." I don't remember who was the manager for Aeolian then, but he didn't think the idea would work. I learned later that he would not approve something unless he could get something for himself out of that idea. How true?

One day I came to Aeolian early, and when I walked into the room, Cook got up and greeted me with, "We have two celebrities in the room." There was another gentleman sitting there, and Cook introduced me to Jan August. Maybe some of you don't remember Jan August, but he was a very good pianist and had a lot of records out. He had a big hit with one called "Misirlou." I've played that number a lot and even used it in some shows. I asked Jan why it sounded like four hands, and he told me that he and his wife did it. I did make a roll of Misirlou. It is QRS no. 7525.

Cook mentioned that he taught Jan August how to play piano years before. He also mentioned that he and Teddy Wilson had a music school in Harlem a lot of years back. Teddy Wilson was the pianist associated with Benny Goodman. I don't remember ever seeing any mention about Cook and Wilson having a school in any write-ups about Cook. I know there are many articles about him, but I don't know why that was never mentioned. Cook also flattered me when he said to Jan, "You have to practice, but Hi never practices." I laughed about it.

I brought up the subject about four hands because I've written four-hand arrangements, and most of my rolls are either three- or four-hand arrangements. With the arranging piano, I could make a piano do what a human being could not do. Celebrity rolls played by certain artists are only two-hand arrangements, while my rolls are more like three and four hands and therefore sound more full. It's like two people playing duets on one piano. It's almost like writing for a large orchestra. As I said before, I once studied symphonic arranging, and I thought I'd apply it to making piano rolls.

Another gimmick I had fun doing was to throw in musical jokes in my arrangements. Unfortunately, I think that only a musician who is familiar with classical, as well as old songs, might appreciate what I added to my arrangements. To give you an illustration, when I did the piano roll of "Ghost Riders in the Sky" for Aeolian#1855, I threw in excerpts from classical selections as a bridge from one chorus to another. For the first transition, I think I used a phrase of *In the Hall of the Mountain King* by Grieg; then the second transition phrase was from *Danse Macabre* by Saint Saens, and the third transition was from the *Sorcerer's Apprentice* by Dukas.

When I did a QRS roll of "Comes Love," QRS10-043, I ended the first phrase with *In the Hall of the Mountain King*—and the end of the second phrase ended with "sixteen tons and what do you get," before the bridge or middle part. If I remember correctly, I also threw in a part of *My Fair Lady*. When I did "For Once in My Life," Aeolian#1923 the ending is the same ending from Liszt's Liebestraume. For me it was fun to listen to, but the average listener will not catch it.

I have to add that I was requested to do "For Once In My Life" for QRS by Ramsi Tick, but he wanted me to do it like the Stevie Wonder record. I didn't want to do it because I felt it was a ballad and not a rythym song. After some wrangling I agreed to do it, but I did the first chorus in rythym like the record and did the second chorus "my way" as a ballad like I did for Aeolian.

When QRS moved to Buffalo, Dick Watson would send a written arrangement to QRS, and Rudy Martin would then cut it. I never sent any written arrangements because going to Buffalo was like taking a mini-vacation. I had friends in Williamsville from the army days. I had mentioned that we were friendly with the Wetzels in Alabama when I was in the army. I found out that Richard Wetzel was killed by a sniper just before he got a furlough to go home; after the war his sergeant, Bill Snow, came to visit Eileen; and they ended up getting married. Then she was Eileen Snow. Sometimes Florrie was with me when I went to Buffalo, and sometimes I was alone. I or we would stay at the Snows' home when I went up to make a piano roll, and they would let me use their car to go to the factory on Niagara Street. Going there was always a pleasure trip for me.

I have a photo of Ramsi Tick meeting me at my plane when I would fly up to Buffalo. Most of my flights were routine, but I had a bit of an incident one night going there. I don't think that engine failure would be classified as an incident. It was a nice evening, and I was enjoying the flight when suddenly there was silence; it was about 6:00 p.m., and it was already dark when it happened. I knew I wasn't far from the airport, but I started to move fast in the cockpit to check things out and try to find the answer.

I have to explain first that when I bought my plane, the former owner told me that the gas gauges were not exact. One always read lower than the other. I really never flew long enough to get that low on fuel. It also seems that the year I bought my plane, the FAA came out with a directive that because someone in a Cessna 172 had an incident, all 172s, instead of flying with the fuel selector set to both (that's the way we were taught), if you were going to fly above five thousand feet, you should either use the right or left fuel tank.

I got into the habit of switching tanks. On most low wing aircraft like the Piper Cherokees I used to fly, you always used either left or right tank. Most low-wing planes use a fuel pump to feed gas to the engine. Most high-wing planes like mine had gravity-fed lines down to the engine. So we did as we were taught or as the FAA said.

On November 22, 1973, I filed a flight plan to Buffalo and listed three and a half hours of fuel on board. My trip to Buffalo from Teterboro usually took two and a half to two and three-quarters hours, so I figured I had enough fuel for the trip. I took off, and when my first checkpoint Wilkes-Barre Scranton came up about ten minutes late, I thought, so what. My next checkpoint Elmira also came up about fifteen minutes late. I was switching tanks while flying and only glancing at the fuel selectors once in a while.

At first I was flying at six thousand five hundred feet, which was the FAA rule for Westerly flight, but at one point I couldn't see out the window and thought my windshield iced up. I happened to look down and saw the ground lights and realized that I was getting into clouds. I dropped down to four thousand five hundred feet where I could see the twinkling lights of the ground below me.

Near Dansville I looked at the right fuel gauge, and it read almost empty, so I switched to the left tank, which read one-quarter full. I was flying along when suddenly it became quiet. I have a yoke mike, so while I was fiddling with the controls to find out what happened, I called Buffalo and told them that I just lost my engine. I asked how far I am from the field, and they said eighteen miles.

I knew that I couldn't glide the eighteen miles, and I knew I was just south of the New York Thruway. If I was close to the Thruway, I'd land on it. That's why I took up gliding at Wurtsboro in Sullivan County, New York. I wanted to know what to do in case of an engine failure. Well, I just had an engine failure, and I trimmed the plane for gliding.

Of course, the old adage for flying is that altitude is insurance for engine failure. The higher you are, the longer you can glide to a safe landing. There was no panic, because panic can kill you, but there was just annoyance in not being able to pinpoint what was wrong and finding the answer.

I have to explain the word "trimming" that I used before. It has nothing to do with decorations. There is a device in the airplane that is a small wheel, which you use to take the pressure out of your control yoke or stick. You can trim the plane to fly with just a light finger pressure. You can trim a plane to fly with your hands off the controls. It is a useful device that you always use.

Meanwhile I'm checking everything in the cockpit. I pushed in the mixture control and pulled the carburetor heat control out in case it was icing. Nothing happened. I tried the primer control because I once read that someone with engine trouble was able to keep priming the engine enough to land. But nothing happened. At one point, the controller at Buffalo asked me, "3500 sierra, what are your intentions?" I wanted to say, "You idiot, (I'm saying it nicely) I want to be able to land safely." I looked out and down, but all I saw was twinkling lights, which I also called fireflies.

I finally reached down and moved the fuel selector to the "both" position, and the engine came back to life. I had trimmed the plane for gliding, and when the engine came back to life, the plane climbed back up. I was already down to about one thousand feet above the ground when that all happened.

To repeat myself in the flying world, altitude is insurance. The higher you are, the longer you can glide. My plane went up to three thousand feet, and I turned north to the Thruway. I asked to be number one to land, and they said I was the only one out there at that time. I got over the Thruway and followed it to the ladder of landing lights for Runway 23 at Buffalo. I landed and had the gas guy fill it up because I wanted to know how much fuel it took. It took thirty-six gallons, which I found out later is needed for level flight. So I came in on just about fumes. Boy, was I lucky!

I want to add that the airplane manufacturers do list the amount of fuel that a plane carries, but I think that it can also fool you. My plane had two 21-gallon tanks, and the fuel cap on the top wing had a notice of 19.5 gallons that was usable. So that meant that I had a capable fuel load of forty-two gallons, but only thirty-nine gallons were usable, yet on the placard next to my seat, it said that only thirty-six gallons were usable in level flight. It reminds me of the automobile placards saying that you could get thirty miles to a gallon, but do you? Boy, was I lucky. I wrote the story of that trip and called it "Assuming Can Be Deadly."

The reason for that title was, I assumed that every time I made the trip from Teterboro to Buffalo, it took me only two and a half to two and three-quarter hours. I didn't stop to think of encountering headwinds for that trip. In reviewing what I did wrong that night, I really got my act together and made it a point to take winds into consideration for all trips in the future. It was something to think about. Boy, did I learn a lesson.

I also realized that another mistake I made was that I didn't take off with full fuel tanks. I had flown for the Civil Air Patrol (CAP) the week before I flew that trip to Buffalo. The CAP had filled my plane with fuel for the return trip from Zahn's Airport out in Long Island to Teterboro. Since it was only a half-hour flight back, I didn't fill my tanks for the flight to Buffalo. I assumed that I had enough gas for the usual trip. That was a mistake. I should have had full tanks of gas before I left. That was stupid! I never made that mistake again.

Another flight that was interesting was after I met Larry Givens. I came up to Cook's room one day, and Cook introduced me to Larry. He heard my roll of "Theme from the Apartment" because Cook had played it for him to show how I could arrange. Larry asked me if I would consider coming out to his home near Butler, Pennsylvania, to make a couple of rolls for his company. Melodee rolls was produced by Larry Givens.

He wanted *Finian's Rainbow* and "Theme from the Apartment." I agreed to go out and do them

I checked my pilot's logbook and found that I flew out to Butler, Pennsylvania, on October 10, 1965, to Larry Given's place. I rented an Alon Aircoupe, which is a low winged two-seater tricycle airplane at Sussex Airport in New Jersey; I put two Stak-Raks in the luggage area as a gift for Larry. It took me three and a half hours to get there because I had rain showers and headwinds along the way. My return flight two days later was only two hours and ten minutes because of a nice tailwind. But that's flying. I had to stay at Larry's home for two days because of the weather.

Using Larry's recording piano was about the same as Cook's piano. The difference was, according to Larry, his machine used a 3-2 punch, where Cook's machine used a 2-1 punch. Of course, the results of a finished roll was the same. I wish I could get my hands on those two rolls, or should I say three rolls, since *Finian's Rainbow* was a medley of two rolls. The recording tape I have of "Theme from the Apartment" that I put on my Volume 5 CD—first selection—is either from the Aeolian roll or from Larry's roll. I don't know.

I was supposed to make a roll of "I Left My Heart in San Francisco" for Larry, and I wrote out the score with all the numbered cues for cutting it, but for some reason, I never made it. I still have the written arrangement to show how I planned that roll with all the numbered punch markings.

I bought my own airplane in 1972. I started to use it, when the weather was good, to fly to Buffalo when I had to go there; but if the weather was bad, I took the airlines, or sometimes I drove there. Only once

The Flying Piano Roll Man

did I have to stop on my way home from QRS to get some sleep, because most of the time, I made those roll arrangements at night at the QRS factory, when I could be alone and not be interrupted by anyone. I stopped one day on the way home near Wilkes-Barre, Pennsylvania, because I was falling asleep while flying; and I didn't want to take any chances. It's a hell of a feeling—falling asleep while flying and waking up to "what happened, and where am I?" It reminded me of the days of the USO tours, where I'd doze off at the wheel, catch it, and have someone else drive. But in flying solo, who's going to take over?

I said before that I liked working at night at QRS when no one was there. I want to add that my method of editing my rolls was sometimes a bit different from using the editing desk. Being alone and having finished my master, I would edit it by rolling out the complete roll on the floor of the factory, and then walk along and read it to see if everything looked OK. I didn't have to unroll or reroll the master like I did on the desk. I could walk up and back and read and reread the master to make sure that it was the way I wanted. If all was OK, then I rolled it up, and I OK'd it for production.

I was asked to make a roll of "It's a Small World" at the request of the Disney company. Since it concerned the World, I brought in my usual ideas of ethnic interludes between each chorus. I used themes like "Mexican" and "Irish" or "Italian and "Isreali" or "Swiss" and "Chinese" to transit from one chorus to another. That's QRS#10-375I. I did get a letter from Disney thanking me for that roll. Now, if I could only find it.

My three year old grandson Richie, from my second marriage, had an operation on his head and we decided to take him to DisneyWorld in Floridaa when he got better. I was looking forward to the trip, since I wanted to visit the exhibit of "Small World" and listen to their version of the song. When we finally got in, and listened, I began to laugh, because what I heard was "my arrangement" of that selection. I guess copying my arrangement was a big flattery to me.

There's a story about my making the piano roll of "New York, New York." This is about the time of the movie *The Godfather* and when Frank Sinatra came out with his rendition of "New York, New York." I think it was about 1973 or 1974. I was up at QRS in August of whichever year it was, and I was there to make the piano rolls of "And I Love Her So" and "Sweet Caroline." I asked Ramsi Tick about making "New York, New York," and his answer was, "Outside of New York who would want that number?"

Most people laugh when I say that, but I do have to explain that I told Ramsi that Sinatra had just come out with that record and I thought it would make a nice roll. Ramsi said no. I did my two rolls and went back home. In late September I took my plane and flew up to Buffalo. Ramsi asked me what I was doing there, and I used that famous phrase from the *Godfather*: "I got an offer you can't refuse." He asked what the offer was, and I said that I would make the piano roll of "New York, New York" for nothing, instead of him having to pay me for the master. He asked what the catch was, and I said that he could give me a royalty for each roll. If I didn't explain before about royalties, I will now.

The roll companies paid about four cents for each roll that was produced. Two cents for music and two cents for words. I asked Ramsi for $.25 for each roll made. He said he would have to talk to his comptroller. I questioned him about him being the boss, but he said he'd have to ask. He came back with "OK, you can make the roll, but there has to be a limit." I asked what's the limit and he said "Three hundred." I laughed because that's what I got for making a master. I went home.

Two weeks later Ramsi called and asked if I could come up and make the roll in time for the Christmas catalog. I told him that I would be up around my birthday on November 9. I came up on the tenth and started to make the roll about 7.00 p.m. I finished it by 7.00 a.m. and made a trial roll of "New York, New York" and took it home. In essence, that roll I forced them to make, became their biggest seller.

PS I don't think I ever got my full royalties of that number.

Another roll I got royalties for was the "Chopsticks Play-Along." I was asked by Ramsi if I could write words for that selection so they could have the usual words on the piano roll. I wrote seven stanzas of words for "Chopsticks," and I was supposed to get two cents royalty for that roll. I laugh and say that I was getting about—are you ready for this answer?—I was making a big six dollars a year! Ha-ha-ha! Again I don't think that I ever kept getting the royalties.

QRS had the celebrity rolls gimmick. One day when I was there to make a roll, Roger Williams was also there to make some rolls. I asked Ramsi, "How about making a Babit and Williams roll," and he said to forget about it. I kept insisting that there were two pianos with marking machines, and we were both there, but Ramsi kept insisting no and finally explained, "You can follow him, but he can't follow you." I realized that we were two different types of players. Roger Williams was a show pianist, while I was an accompanist pianist. We had two different styles of playing. Williams played piano with an orchestral background, while I played mostly single piano using melody, rhythm, and full harmony chord sounds.

When I'm playing with a band and I don't have to play the rhythm, I can do solo fill-ins. I can run up and down the piano like Williams or any other soloist that plays with an orchestra. Then again, I'm used to playing for a lot of singers and dancers, which is a bit different than playing with a band group. There are different ways of playing, according to the situation.

Also in my favor is that I have and use the big-hand stretches to get the sounds of a stretched glee club choir. I also have arthritis in my fingers and make it a point to move around the piano to exercise them. In so doing, I use scales and arpeggios to fill in when the melody stops in the selections. This of course makes me a bit different in playing piano, but it doesn't make me better than some others. I have my style, and other piano players have their style. It's like composers whose style you can tell if you listen to a lot of music, whether it be classical or popular.

I'm sure if you listen to a lot of music you can recognize the styles of Gershwin, Berlin, Cole Porter, or Beethoven, Tschaikovsky, Chopin, etc. It may be a little more difficult to recognize the latest type of composers because in my opinion, they write songs today based on words, not melodic lines, like in the '30s and '40s. The old Broadway shows had melodic passages with ranges that would show off a singer's voice, and they had more of a story to tell. Today's music, I believe, is based on lyrics that use only the same repeated phrases with loud entertainers jumping all over the stage so that you can't hear your partner's voice next to you.

I mentioned Roger Williams before. I also met with Liberace in Las Vegas one year when I went out there to gamble a bit. I was already remarried, and when I told Ramsi Tick that I was going to Las Vegas, he told me to look up Liberace and tell him that I'm from QRS. Liberace had just made some celebrity rolls for QRS. When I got to Vegas, we went to see him perform. I think it was at the Hilton Hotel. After the show I told Marilyn that I want to go backstage and see Liberace, but she declined and said that she'd rather play the slot machines. I went backstage by myself. He asked me why it took so long, almost six months, to get his rolls; and I had to explain to him that he used the marking machine, while I used a different type of machine.

I had to explain that when you use a marking machine, you first have to give the marked paper roll to someone in the factory to hand cut each line and space. I told him that I used a slow punching unit to make my piano roll and that I could make my first master in one day or two. I could then edit it right away and be able to produce the final piano roll in just a couple of days. He thanked me for the info, and he accepted the reason for the months of delay of his rolls. That was the difference between celebrity rolls and machine-arranged rolls.

During my run of making piano rolls, I would occasionally tape some and also started keeping a collection of every roll I made. I made about three hundred fifty rolls between QRS, Aeolian, and Melodee. Of course, I stored them in my Stak-Raks. How convenient! That whole collection was stored in the basement of the house I lived in on Staten Island, New York. When I made less and less rolls and finally stopped, I was still busy with the Irish steak house in the Bronx and busy with teaching and piano tuning

There was a time, while I was playing at Donaghy's in the Bronx, that I tried to give myself a younger appearance. I had some hairpieces made and even grew a moustache. One night I told my wife, Marilyn, to meet me outside the steak house. I had the new hairpiece on, and she didn't recognize me, even though I was standing next to her. I have some photos of me with that hairpiece, and I still laugh about it.

I have, on my tapes of the Donaghy organ playing, a lot of original music that I've never put on paper; but I did manage to write some scores to include with this book. When this book is finished, my next chore will be to write the rest of the unfinished songs and get them out so that I can have a better collection of them. I will make lead sheets of my originals and add them to the book. A lead sheet consists of one line (staff) with the notes and chord names above it and with the words underneath the notes. For those of you who can read music, you may appreciate my music add-ons! I may still go back to writing full arrangements (both hands), but I'd have to write it so that the average person can play it. I can't write it the way I play it because I use the tenths. You will see that I arranged with some of the tricks I do.

On Thanksgiving Day in 1992, I developed a back problem, and after going through some visits with chiropractors, I was sent to a hospital for CAT scans and found out that I had herniated discs. I was then sent to see a back surgeon in New York Hospital, who thought that there was only a fifty-fifty chance that surgery would help and that my problem should heal up in a few months. Since we had a trip planned for December 29, 1992, to visit with my brother in sunny Florida, we thought we'd have to postpone that trip; but the doctor advised me to go, get into the pool, and that should help me to get better sooner.

We came down December 29 to stay at Century Village in Deerfield Beach. I was taken off the airplane in a wheelchair. I tried swimming, and it started to help me. Two weeks later on January 16, I carried my bags, got back on the plane, and I've worked ever since. By Sunday of that arrival week, I told Marilyn that I was going to rent a car. She questioned me about my driving ability and I said that I just have to move my ankles. We decided to look for a place and move to Florida because she had just been told that after thirty-two years of being the head bookkeeper for her firm, she was being retired. We were then living in Staten Island, New York. We found a house for rent in Tamarac, and we decided to move there. We moved in May or June of 1993. We moved to the Mainlands of Tamarac, and our house area was called Section Eight. Army people would get a laugh because in army lingo, a section eight discharge was for mental disability. Ha-ha!

I made my next mistake, which I didn't realize for another five years. I went and sold my whole collection of piano rolls and Stak-Raks to a customer of mine on Staten Island, who told me that he was going to put them on computer floppy disks. This was before CDs became big. I sold my whole collection because I had no room for it at the new place in Florida. Also since I was out of the piano-roll-making business and I didn't even have a player piano anymore, I would sell it all, including the Stak-Raks and some rolls I made that were never in the catalog or on the market. The person that I sold my collection to told me that being in the computer business, he would put my rolls on floppies, and this would help to preserve them. He never did.

We moved in the spring of 1993 to Tamarac, Florida, and set up home there. While living in Tamarac, I found work with a piano dealer in Miami. The dealer's name was Victor's Pianos. I started to build up my piano-tuning business. I was with Victor for a year or so, and then left him and went to work for Bobb's Pianos, who had stores in Hallandale (main office) and in Oakland Park, a suburb of Fort Lauderdale and closer to my home in Tamarac. In 1996, my landlord did us a favor by telling us that he had to sell the house because he was getting a divorce.

I had a customer in Wynmoor (a condo development), and after calling her, she told me to come and look at the bulletin board for vacancies. That was on a Sunday. I went and took two names, called Sunday night, and made appointments for the next day to see the both apartments. Monday morning we went and saw the first one, which was a two-story walk-up with small rooms. Then we went to the next one, which is where I live now, and we made a deal and moved there in June of 1996. So my old landlord did me a big favor by having to get a divorce. The favor was that my wife Marilyn had been stuck in the house, because we had only one auto, and I was using it to do my piano tuning, etc. When we moved to Wynmoor, there were plenty of things for her to do while I was on the road.

When we moved to Wynmoor in the town of Coconut Creek in June of 1996, I picked up the local condo paper and looked through it. I saw a blurb about music and piano playing. I called about it and was invited to a rehearsal of a talent group. We went to the rehearsal of that group, and sat in the audience. When I was asked to come up to the stage and play for one of the singers, I went and, as usual, I asked the singer what Key she was going to sing in. That's when I know if the singer is a real singer. A professional singer always know what Key they sing in. The singer didn't know, so I told her to sing and that I would pick up her Key.

Sitting next to Marilyn was someone who said to her that I didn't belong to that group, but I should be with his group. His name is Mel Goldberg and he is a saxophone player. After that short rehearsal he approached me and asked me to come the following Monday to his rehearsal. I did. I became the music director for a couple of shows. That first group was called the "Mildred Levine's Follies", and I did a few shows for her. That second group on the following Monday was called the "Gertrude Weinberg's Dance Group" and we put on shows every two years since 1998. I'm rehearsing them for another show in March 2011.

At the first show that I did, some people in the audience came to me and asked me about playing for their shows in Century Village in Boca Raton at the

Beth Shalom Temple. I did two shows a year for them for about eight or nine years. The two shows were for Chanukah and for Purim, two Jewish Holidays. Then a condo that is just north of us, called the Township, hired me to be the music director for some of their shows. I just finished a show there. It's nice to get word-of-mouth recognition!

On one of the shows that I did for the dance troupe, I had to do some original-music writing. It was a show called a *Trip around the World* where we played a lot of ethnic music. When we did the French trip, I was asked if I knew of a different "Can-Can" than the one that Offenbach wrote. I thought of something, and I started playing. The sax man and guitar player looked at me and laughed because they knew I would rattle off something. I went into a two-part selection, and when the choreographer asked me for the name, I said, "I just made it up." You will find it in the list of music that I'm adding at the end of the book. I just call it "Can-Can." I also wrote an Israeli number for the trip to Israel part of the show. I may develop that Israeli selection into a rhapsody. It's fun and easy for me to compose music.

In September of that year of 1993, just after I moved to Tamarac from Staten Island, Dorothy Bromage called me from Boston, Massachusetts, to tell me that I was going to become an honorary member of AMICA. AMICA is the Automatic Musical Instrument Collectors Association. AMICA is involved with player pianos and music boxes. I was flattered for that honor and thought nothing more of it. I used to get mailings for their conventions, but I didn't feel it necessary to go since I didn't know anyone there.

The Flying Piano Roll Man

In 1997, Dorothy Bromage called me again to say that I was being invited to their next convention in Sandusky, Ohio. I didn't want to go because I still didn't know anyone there, and I was busy tuning and playing here in Florida. My wife insisted I go because I already had the tickets. I flew up to Cleveland, where I was picked up by three gentlemen who told me that they were taking me as their guest for dinner. I think it was the Leedy brothers who picked me up at the airport.

As we're riding in the car, they put a tape in, and I hear that it's me being interviewed by a CBS reporter at the Imperial Industries in the Bronx factory in 1965. They had memorabilia that I never thought of getting and saving. When we got to the hotel and checked in, I heard, "Hi, Babit's here," and I'm thinking, "So what?" After coming down for dinner, everyone wanted to meet me. Later when I went into the hospitality room, I was asked to play the piano, and it became an every-night thing. They brought me piano rolls to be autographed, and I had to go buy some felt pens, since the plain ballpoints wouldn't write on the roll paper. I called my wife and told her what happened and that I suddenly felt like I was a celebrity. But my hat still fits on my head!

The routine for the conventions, which is usually five days, was normally check-in on Wednesday, tours and a show on Thursdays, more tours on Fridays, and a pumper contest on Friday night. Saturdays was for selling at the mart, and a show and dinner Saturday night. On Sunday, there was the big breakfast get-together, and then either you went on more tours or you traveled home.

Hi Babit

On Thursday night they had John Arpin from Canada entertaining. He was very good, but he played mostly jazz piano. I asked him why he didn't play more ragtime for this type of audience. He played mostly his concert tour music. On Saturday we had William Bolcomb and his wife doing an 1890s type of show. After watching those shows, I thought that I would talk to Mike Walters about doing a better show for AMICA.

I mentioned to Mike that I could possibly do a show for the AMICAns that would be more appropriate for their enjoyment by explaining how I made and what went into making piano rolls. He said that he would take it under advisement. He did invite me and my wife to the next convention, which took place in 1998 at the Sheraton Hotel in the Niagara Falls section of Canada. At the conventions I made friends with a lot of people and still keep in touch with them.

I didn't do a show at Niagara, but I did a lot of piano playing there and autographing piano rolls. We took a tour to the QRS factory, which was only nineteen or twenty miles from our hotel. The piano that I used to make the roll masters on was now in an enclosed room, like a museum piece with a mannequin sitting at the piano. There was a big picture window showing the piano. They insisted that I take some photos in front of that piano. It sure brought back memories. I also made a master on the recording piano that they used for the celebrities. I never did anything with that master, because it was only a two-hand arrangement, and I would rather make my usual three- and four-hand arrangements. I tried to get QRS to give me their computer program so that I could make some arrangements at home, but they declined.

I recently found out that I was on YouTube with a video of my piano playing at the 1998 convention. I went to the next year's 1999 convention, which was in Boston, and did the same routine of playing piano and autographing piano rolls. There was a long hiatus before I got my next invitation, which was to the Woodland Hills Convention in 2008 in California. I asked my sister Roz if she would like to go to that convention. She agreed and thought that she was going to see some small music boxes and a few player pianos. She was flabbergasted by what she saw and raved about it to everyone when we returned. She learned about orchestrions and players.

I must have been a hit, because there were a lot of write-ups of my appearance and performance there. They were on the MMD Internet display and the AMICA bulletin periodical. I want to thank Frank and Shirley Nix and Terry Smythe for their nice comments.

I was invited to the 2009 Convention in Cinncinati, Ohio. Roz and I had a great time with the tours and the shows. I'm invited to the next convention in Buffalo in July 2010. It will be like old home week being up in Buffalo again. I have wonderful memories of that area. Like I said before, Florrie and I used to visit with the Snow family in Williamsville, a suburb of Buffalo, long before I began to travel to the QRS factory. Florrie would occasionally go with me when I had to make some piano rolls at QRS, until she passed away in 1974. On most of the trips, Florrie and I would stay at the Snow residence. Sometimes we would stay at a motel. Marilyn never went with me to QRS when I had to go there to make rolls.

On one trip, Florrie and I stayed at a motel. While eating one night at the motel restaurant, I went to the piano where some girl was playing and watched her. There suddenly was a commotion near the bar, and the pianist seemed to want to go there. I offered to sit in for her, and when I said I did play, she got up. I played for about a half hour till the other pianist came back. I did have a crowd around me. I got into the habit of going with Florrie to eat in that restaurant after I would come back from QRS. I also invited the Snows to join us at that eatery for dinner. I played there almost every night, and when we checked out at the end of our stay, the management refused to charge us. Sometimes it pays to play randomly. You never know what it brings.

Now I'd like to talk about how I got involved with making CDs. I was fixing a grand piano a few years ago, and while I was working on the action of the grand, I heard piano playing on the customer's sound system. I thought, "That's a player-piano sound," and then came the dawn, and I said, "Hey! That's my piano roll. Where'd you get it?" The customer came out laughing and said it was my roll of "Black Bottom Stomp." I asked him how I could get to hear it on my computer, and he said that all you have to do is to go to Google and type in "Hi Babit music rolls." Then up comes a few pages with my name. One of the selections that was on that page was marked "ragtime classics free download." If you highlight that selection, you get a page in German, with about fifty or sixty listings of piano rolls; and if you scan down, you come to the title "Black Bottom Stomp" and my name, Hi Babit. If you click on the square in front, it starts playing the selection. I went home and tried it on my computer. It worked, and I went to Danny's Pianos to tell him about it.

Danny Geoghegan, who co-owns Danny's Piano & Organ Company with his brother Gerry, is an electronics genius. He has a piano dealer's store on West Copans Road in Pompano Beach, Florida. I spend a lot of time there because I tune all his pianos. He built a special device to copy my piano rolls. He used an Ampico player unit with an electronic reader to produce my first two CDs. When the machine started to malfunction, I went to a customer's home where there was a player piano that I just tuned and asked to let me tape my piano rolls there.

I was given permission and came with my tape recorder. I taped more piano rolls and made two more CDs that I sold or gave out at the conventions. Then I found more old tapes of the recordings I made years ago of each of most of my rolls. I made another volume 5, which I call my favorites, because it has some of my better roll arrangements on it. It seems that, little by little, I had acquired a lot of my piano rolls these past few years; and I was able to decide, between my tapes or the piano rolls I acquired, which selections I should put on a CD.

I bought a machine that copies either LPs or tapes to CD blanks. I found that I could make my own CDs and started making them and selling them. Sometimes I gave some out to friends and customers. I also found old tapes of my days at the Donaghy's Steak House in the Bronx, New York. I made some CDs of my steak house days and from a cruise I made in 1975. As I said earlier, when you play with a band, you are free to really move around the piano. When you play solo, you have to have a different style. I also found the tape of Larry Johnson and me doing a duo organ and piano tape. I think that between all those types of CDs, you can hear the different styles of my playing. The steak house CD is mostly Hammond organ, with a lot of my early compositions. I have a CD of the band I led on that 1975 cruise of the SS Victoria.

I would like to add at this time, since I mentioned Danny's Pianos, that I composed a tango when I was at Donaghy's Restaurant, and the Latin name for it was "Lagrimas de mi amor" and in English, "Tears of My Love." I wrote the lyrics in English, and when I started to work for Danny about 1996, he had his daughter translate my English lyrics to Spanish. Now I have them in both. At a birthday party for Danny a couple of years ago, I met an Argentine singer who heard about the tango; and when I played it for her, she asked for a copy. Well, I've been remiss in not writing out that arrangement for her. She wanted to use it in her shows. That's another chore I have to get to. Maybe that song will give me some future recognition.

Danny rents out pianos, and I have to go and tune the pianos at the client's place. A couple of years ago, Danny rented a piano that had to be delivered to the Marriot Hotel on A1A in Fort Lauderdale. I got there as they were setting up the piano. I went through the ballroom where there was a bandstand with a piano on it, but Gerry told me that I was to tune the piano in the hallway. While I was tuning that piano, someone came and asked when I'm going to tune the piano in the ballroom. I told him that I was only hired to tune the hallway piano. They asked if I would tune the ballroom piano if they paid me for it. Of course, I replied.

As soon as I finished tuning, I went inside the ballroom and got up on the stage. A young fellow was standing there and asked who I was. I said that I'm the tuner. He asked for my name; and when I said, "Hi Babit," he looked at me and said, "Stop joshing me, what's your name?" I pulled out my cards and showed him. His question (which I've heard before) was, "Are you the real Hi Babit?" When I said yes, he tells me that he has all my rolls at home. His name is Michael Andrew, and he is an entertaining singer. The next January he gave me four tickets to see his show at the Boca Pops Orchestra show. He told me to see him backstage after the show. I went to see him, and he brought four rolls for me to autograph! He kept telling everyone who I am and what I did. He was the entertainer, but he was touting me. What a laugh!

I think that I've given you enough information of what I have been doing these past eighty some odd years. Now I can go back to working on my compositions, rehearsals, piano tunings, and inventions. I think that if I keep busy enough, it will keep me alive to do more. I believe in keeping the brain working. I will try to find photos and other memorabilia to include with this story, which might help in making the reading more palatable, understandable, and enjoyable. I will add some original music and include it in the appendix.

I did try to buy back my whole collection of piano rolls and the stak-raks, but I didn't have any success. I called the person that I sold the collection to, but he never answered me. After a few attempts to reach him, I was told that the entire collection was sold to someone, but I was not told to whom. I even put a blurb in the MMD Internet column to inquire about who bought my entire collection. No one ever called me. I'm still willing to buy it back.

 I have to finish this chapter by saying that I just came back from the Buffalo convention, and I had a great time there. The tours were great, and I even won a couple of bucks in the Niagara casino. We had fun in the hospitality room at night, and it just great fun!

Chapter 6

The Flying Years

I think I was always intrigued with speed. I mentioned earlier that I would go to the Floyd Bennett Field for the three-dollar sightseeing flights and later on with the motorcycles. I don't know if it was the speed or fast movement that got my adrenalin going, but I always seemed to be on the move. Maybe there was the excitement of danger! Who knows? But I finally decided in 1957 to go after flying.

I went to Middletown, New York, and got my first flying lesson in a Piper Cub. According to my pilot's logbook (yes, I still have it), that was July 11, 1957. When Florrie found out about it, she got mad and made me promise not to pursue flying. She thought it was dangerous, but I figured I would wait for the right time to do it. It came a few years later.

In 1959 we moved from Clarkson Avenue in Brooklyn to Flushing, Queens. I think the address was 4240 Bowne Street. In a way, it was closer to my running to Yonkers, to the Balalaika restaurant, and we thought a move would be good for us. I think there's a saying about making a change for the better. In May of 1960, Florrie and I decided to take a trip out west to California where Florrie's friend Bella lived. I think it was Glendale, California. My drummer Vinnie also decided to make that same trip because he had relatives living out there. We thought we'd drive to the West Coast. We left in his 1957 Plymouth discussing the route we would take.

I wanted to go south toward Alabama where I was once stationed at Fort McClellan, near Anniston, and then head west through Lousiana, Texas, etc. I think we stopped in New Orleans for some sightseeing. It was quite a trip. It took us two to three days just to cross Texas. Florrie stayed in California, and I went back to New York to work. Florrie came back home about November, and I had a surprise for her. She wasn't too happy when she found out that I had my pilot's license. She was slow accepting the fact that I intended to fly. But slowly she started to go on flights with me, like she used to go riding on my motorcycles. Years later when I had my own plane, I took her and her eighty-five-year-old mother flying. Things change!

Flushing had a small airport, and it was only about ten minutes from our apartment. I went there one day, July 6, 1960, according to my logbook, and started again to take flying lessons. It was, again, a Piper Cub, which is a two-place tandem seater. We went out along the north shore of Long Island, and on the way back, the instructor asked me to move a lever on the left side of the plane. When I asked him what that lever was for, he replied that I would read it in the book.

The Flying Piano Roll Man

I didn't teach music by telling my students to read the instructions in the book, and I said good-bye to that instructor. It just happened that about that same time, I went to an affair of a musician's friend of mine, who was having a bar mitzvah for his son. At the affair, I met an old friend, Hal Silvers, another accordion player; and when I mentioned that I started taking flying lessons, he advised me to stick to flying seaplanes. He said that it was safer. You could, in an emergency, land on those big floats and walk away. He recommended that I go to the Pelham seaplane base in the Bronx, because he once had a seaplane and based it there.

That seaplane base was only about twenty minutes from the Balalaika restaurant, and so I went there. That was July 13, 1960. I started flying a Luscombe, two-place, high wing sixty-five horsepower seaplane, which had no radio or self-starter. Seating inside it was like sitting in a bathtub with your legs stretched out. I had to use pillows to get to see out the front window. To start the plane, I had to first stand on the float, hold onto the strut of the wing, lean forward, and hand prop the engine. Once the engine started, I got into the plane, but someone had to hold it in place before I could start to taxi or move out to the bay for the takeoff. When you move an aircraft on the ground or water, you call it taxiing. You taxi a plane to go get fuel or to go to the runway for the takeoff, or departure.

I had a good instructor; I'm trying to decipher the signature of that instructor, and it looks like E. S. Pulko. The plane number was N45850. I wonder where that plane is today. Is it still in service? I was flying almost three to four times a week. At that time, the Throggs Neck Bridge was being built, and we would sometimes take off toward that bridge. On a lot of takeoffs, the instructor would pull back the throttle and say that we just lost the engine and had to make an emergency landing. I have to add that you could pull that trick on seaplanes because you always had plenty of water to land on. I wouldn't try that stunt when you are using a land plane, because when you take off from an airport that's based on land, you have little choices to make for emergency landings because of all the residential areas

On July 25, 1960, I finally soloed. That was after twenty-six hours of dual instruction. In those days, when someone first soloed, they would, if on land planes, cut off a piece of their shirttail; but on seaplanes, they threw you into the water after you soloed. Which is what happened to me. I have that photo of me in the water next to the plane. What I did then was to take off my clothes, hang them on all the props of the planes, and go flying in my underwear.

Of course, on my first solo, my engine conked out when I landed. I got out on the float and tried to start it but couldn't. One of the employees came out in a motorboat and asked me look at the fuel selector, which was situated next to my left foot. It seems I accidentally shut the fuel selector when I landed. I opened the valve, started the engine, took off, and completed the usual three takeoffs and landings to get my student license. What a feeling! You could feel the difference from flying solo or with the instructor. It was a quicker takeoff. The plane was lighter. I think that I should mention what it cost, in those days, to fly. You may not believe it, but the charge for dual instruction on the seaplane was only sixteen dollars an hour, and solo flying was only eleven dollars an hour. Not in today's time!

That week, the Balalaika closed for a summer's vacation. Some musician friends asked me if I could go to New Jersey to audition for a job in a new motel called the Fountains. It was in Long Branch, New Jersey. I went with them, and we got the job, and they gave us rooms. The manager told me later that it was because of me that they got the job. They had a new piano and organ, and they liked my playing of both.

I went looking for a seaplane base, but New Jersey will not allow seaplanes on lakes, only on tidewater. I went to the Monmouth County Airport and got into a 150 Cessna, two-place airplane, which had a radio, self-starter, and a one hundred horsepower engine. What a difference. I flew that plane, and then went the same day to the Red Bank airport where they had a Piper Tri-Pacer, four-place airplane, with one hundred fifty horsepower, and a radio. After flying that one, I made up my mind to stick with the Tri-Pacer. That was August 3, 1960. Red bank airport (now gone) was only fifteen minutes from the motel. It was quick and easy to get to. I want to say again what the charges were for the flying. Dual instruction was twenty dollars an hour and solo fifteen dollars hourly.

Again I had a good instructor, Larry Schofield, and he would put me through all kinds of maneuvers to give me good instruction and really put me on the ball. He would put a visor on me so that I could see only the instrument panel and not the outside view. Then he asked me to close my eyes, and he would put the airplane in all kinds of gyrations called unusual attitudes and say, "Open your eyes and use the instruments to get the airplane to fly straight and level."

Sometimes you do miss some instructions by assuming it's easy to understand, like learning to fly cross country using the omni radio. Larry told me to keep the needle of the radio device centered when going cross country. But he omitted one little bit of advice, or I didn't hear him explain it. When I had to do my triangular cross country over a hundred miles, which was a requirement for my license, I found out the correct way to use the omni. I learned the hard way!

I left Red Bank and flew to Hanover, New Jersey. From there I had to fly to Easton, Pennsylvania. I took off, set my course for Easton, and blithely flew along. I noticed the needle of the omni radio moving to the left, so I moved the needle back to the center. I kept flying, and again the needle moved to the left, and again I centered it. Then I began checking my air map with the terrain below, and to my surprise and chagrin, it didn't match. According to the map, the Easton Airport was about five miles due west of the S-turns in the Delaware River, and I was way north of there. I made a change of direction to get to that S-turns area.

The flight manual said that Easton had all-way runway landings, and I thought I would see about four runways. Well, I turned west from the S-turns and figured that in four to five minutes, I would be there, but all I saw were fields and fields. I saw a plane below me and started following him. I realized that I was heading too far west and went back to the S-turns in the Delaware River and started again. This time I went lower and slower and finally saw a building with "Easton" marked on it. It was a big grass field, and I realized that you could land in any direction, according to what the winds were. For your information, you always take off and land into the wind. The heading into the wind will give you lift on takeoff, and heading into the wind for landing will slow you down. I tried to give you a simple explanation.

I landed, and there was a gentleman sitting under a tree smoking a pipe. He remarked, "Saw you coming over about twenty minutes ago." I did some explanations about my trying to use the omni, and he then explained that when the needle moves away from the center after you have set the course, all you do is turn to the direction of that needle movement and keep flying until the needle comes back to center, and you are back on the right course. If Larry had explained it to me, I forgot and won't make that mistake again. I had my logbook signed to keep my trip recorded for the license.

I accomplished all my requisites for the license. I did my air work, passed my written tests, and was ready for the flight test. On October 5, 1960, I passed my flight test on the first attempt. I had heard that pilots sometimes had to take more than one test to pass and get their license. Now I'm a private pilot.

According to my logbook, it seems that it only took me two months to get my private pilot license. Wow! In reviewing my logbook, I seemed to have done a lot of flying with different types of planes and flew to various destinations. I think I'll add that when the summer job at the Fountains Motel was over, and I was back in Queens; I was commuting to the Red Bank airport for my flying hours and tests.

In reviewing my logbook number 1, I see that my flying continued out of Red Bank airport for the remainder of

1960. In 1961, I started alternating between seaplanes and wheel planes, and finding different airports to fly out of. With the seaplanes, I was either flying out of Pelham, where I started, or flying out of Little Ferry in New Jersey, or from suburban out of Long Beach, New York. I see that I got my seaplane endorsement or rating at suburban on January 16, 1962. I flew out of City Island in the Bronx area a few times and from Searingtown on Long Island, which was like a country club. I believe that all the seaplane bases that I flew out of in the New York area are now long gone.

Flying seaplanes gave me some insights into improving my wheel flying. If any of you are interested in flying, my recommendations are to take up flight instruction in seaplanes for gaining some skills that you won't get on wheel planes. One of the most important skills to learn is glassy-water landings. That is a term used for landing on still smooth water where you can't tell where the top of the water is. The trick is to make your landings with a little power and a bit of nose-up attitude, like getting into a stall position; and as you keep slowly moving back your power and getting lower, you wait for the feel of the pontoons of your plane touching the water, and you know then that you are landed. I used that type of glassy-water landings for night landings, and it usually made for a smooth touchdown. It not only makes you feel good, but it sure impresses your passengers.

There is a saying about flying by the seat of your pants. Well, I have to admit that between my seaplane instructor and the Red Bank instructor, I learned to fly by the seat of my pants. I learned to fly by the feel, sounds, looks (scanning), and intuitions. It was drilled into me; and even today, when I'm flying in an airliner, I can tell what the pilot is doing. It is something you don't forget.

On one airliner flight I felt that we were landing a bit fast (we call it "hot"), and when I was getting off the plane, the pilots were standing at the door of the cockpit, and one of the pilots was a female. She was the captain. When I got in front of her near the exit, I said to her, "You came in a bit hot, didn't you?" She looked surprised and said somewhat sheepishly, "It happens sometimes." I didn't berate her, I just mentioned it. I can usually tell the hotshot pilots from the old timers.

In June of 1961, I joined the Allied Flyers Club at Deer Park, out at the east end of Queens. I checked out flying airplanes in almost every airport around New York. I wanted to try all the different airplanes that I could so that no matter where I went, I could rent an airplane and go flying. I also flew from airports with only grass runways, which could be slightly different than paved runways. I have endorsements for almost every type of two-, three-, or four-seater airplanes there were at that time. Sometimes I got free flights when I went shopping for an aircraft. I always thought of buying an airplane in those days, so when I got my patent in 1972, I did buy one.

Trying to find time between my piano tuning, music teaching, band playing, and flying kept me very busy. Most of the airports that I flew from are now long gone. They became either malls or developments for housing projects. Roosevelt Field of Lindbergh's time is a very big mall. Deer Park became a housing development. That's what happened to a lot of the airports I used to fly out of.

Hi Babit

I joined the Civil Air Patrol (CAP) where I thought I would get more flying without spending too much money. While with the CAP, I latched on to another invention. I went to a meet at Atlantic City, New Jersey, and they said we were to fly in to Bader Field and to bring your own tie-downs. In case the average layman doesn't know, airplanes are parked by tying them down to an anchor in the ground so that winds don't blow them around or damage them. They use either ropes or chains that tie to a cast concrete anchor in the ground with a protruding ring, or to a stretched rope that is also anchored down to the ground.

At Bader Field I found that the ground was asphalt and that there were no tie-down facilities to accommodate our group of flyers. I found that when flying to different airports, they didn't always have tie-down facilities for transient flyers. What they had on the market were tie-down kits that had either stakes or screw-type devices for hammering or screwing into the ground, and then tying the plane to those stakes. People who go camping know what I mean about using screw-in stakes for tents. If the ground is soft due to rains, or just plain grass, I don't believe those tie-downs would hold well in the event of a strong storm.

I read reports about those types of tie-downs. I received a copy of *Aviation Consumer*, and they did a report on airplane tie-downs. They hoped that some inventor would come up with a better device than what they have at present. I think I will write them and tell them that I have that type of device. Maybe this time I will have some success.

My patent was named "Securing Devices for Aircraft." It is a set of three portable telescoping stands to attach to the tie-down rings of any aircraft and secure it for insurance against most type of winds. The patent was issued in 1972. Of course, I wouldn't guarantee the device in hurricane or tornado areas. I tried to get one company to carry my units in the plane like you carry an emergency jack in the car. If you fly someplace and they don't have tie-down facilities for your aircraft, all you have to do is pull out my device, originally named "tylok," then later changed to "Tysafe," and attach it to the tie-down rings of your aircraft. I like to play with names, and I thought that "Tysafe" could be turned around to spell "safe-ty" or "safety" as a catchy title. I always had fun playing with names to suit the device.

As I said once before, inventing can sometimes escalate into a more involved process. When I first showed my device to the CAP at a meet at Zahn's Airport, one of the members asked me if I was going for lunch; and when I asked him why he asked, he said that I may not find it when I returned. Now I had to figure out a way to safeguard my unit and had to come up with locking devices. That's how you can get more involved with inventing. I invented locks that could work but were not really practicable. I finally came up with a simpler design in my later prototypes. I did away with internal locking devices and redesigned my invention to just use padlocks you can buy at stores.

As an inventor, you can get carried away with ideas, and you can overinvent. I have to interject here that in making piano rolls, you can also overarrange by putting in too many holes; too many holes can result in losing the air to sound the notes. I had sixteen attachments for my device. It had tripod legs with slides and toes, etc. When I got the patent in 1972, I knew I couldn't use someone else's plane to demonstrate it, so I went and bought a 1964 Cessna Skyhawk, also called a 172, with the call number N3500S (Sierra).

I was going to fly out to San Diego, California, to demonstrate my new parking device at the AOPA Plantation Party show in 1973. I was an AOPA member (AOPA stands for Aircraft Owners and Pilots Association). The AOPA had a show every year called the Plantation Party where they would show the new airplanes and devices on the market for the flying public. The Plantation Party was in a different section of the country each year. I belonged to a few aero clubs before I bought my plane and was able to get experience in different types of aircraft through the club memberships.

I wanted cleaner models than I had made to show at that show, so I went to a machine shop in Lower Manhattan and showed them what I wanted. I explained that I'm a musician and not a machinist. Although I made the prototypes myself in a friend's machine shop in Queens, I wanted a clean model. Well, they made the newer models with a few mistakes, and when I asked what it would cost for a set of three units (every plane has three tie-down rings, one under each wing and one under the tail), they told me the price; I told them that I wanted to sell the complete kit for that price, and they explained that they had sixteen castings to drill and attach. So I had over-invented and decided to redo everything. However, I was determined to show what I had at the AOPA Plantation Party celebration. I corrected and cleaned up my units and got ready to leave for San Diego.

The Flying Piano Roll Man

On September 10, 1973, I started out late from Teterboro Airport where I was parked for ten years. I want to add that I tied my plane there to a rope in the ground. On stormy days, I would go out and use my device and noticed that while my plane stood still like it was a building without moving, the other planes were bobbing up and down like boats on the water in a storm. I felt that I had a workable and useful system.

I left quite late, and by the time I reached the area of Luray, Virginia. it was getting dark, and I landed at the Luray Airport. I was about to experience the famous southern hospitality. No one answered the radio calls that I made to the airport, but, as I came in for a landing, the landing lights came on. There was no one at the office, but there was a lit phone. I called, and someone came and took me to a motel and closed my flight plan. They told me to call them in the morning. I did, and they picked me up and took me to the Luray Caverns for breakfast and told me to call them when I finished. When I asked what my charges were for staying overnight and all the pickups, they said that I owed them only $1.50 for overnight parking. Wow!

They didn't have my type of gas and advised me to fly only ten miles to the Shenandoah airport to fill up. I went there, and then started for my next leg to Knoxville, Tennessee. I landed there for gas and for lunch. They took me by van to a diner and said to call them for the return. They only charged me for the gas, no landing fee. I took off for my next leg, but having a medium-speed plane, I reached Nashville; as it was getting dark and not knowing the area, I landed there and decided to stay overnight. There was a Hilton Hotel on the field, and they sent a car for me. The bill at the Hilton was only seventeen dollars. In the morning, it was a little foggy, but they drove me back to the Cessna dealer where I parked my plane overnight, and the charges were only for gas and $1.50 for parking. Wow! If I sound too technical in my explanations of flying or music, please forgive. That's me! The prices today will never compare with those of yesteryear.

I took off and climbed between mounds of clouds that looked like giant snowbanks, and I was sorry I didn't have my movie camera with me. What a scene that would have made. I flew along, crossed the famous Mississippi River, and decided to land at Jonesboro, Arkansas, since the air map indicated they had a flight service station there, and I figured they would have a place to eat. As they say in Brooklyn, "fuggettaboutit." I was in a different world. They said I was on my own to get into town to eat. I finally got a ride. The town was a typical western town, with one-story buildings, and the men wore the big hats. I ate in a small place, and when I asked about how to get back to the airport, they all shrugged and ignored me. I guess I looked like an alien.

I finally got a ride back to the airport, and when I visited the flight service station and mentioned about where I wanted to fly, they informed me that there were heavy thunderstorms along my route and that I'm better off going to Memphis, Tennessee, which was only sixty miles away; and I could catch an airliner to go to the West Coast. So I flew to Memphis and parked my plane with the Cessna people there. They gave me a lift to the terminal with my device and bags, and I took American Airlines to San Diego. While flying, I noticed that flight service was right—I saw the thunderstorm buildups that were higher than our altitude, and we were at about thirty-eight thousand feet altitude. I was glad that I listened to their advice.

At the show, I showed the Cessna company people my device, and they liked the idea, but my request for them to put it on each aircraft as optional equipment was denied. They said that if I could prove that the public wanted that device, then they would take it on. I told them that if the public wanted it, I didn't need them.

I flew back to Memphis after the show to retrieve my plane, and when I asked them for the charges, they said I only owed them fourteen dollars for parking for the week. I flew home, and about a week later, I flew up to Monticello in Sullivan County in Upstate New York and landed at the small airport to make a phone call. I was told that before I could make that phone call, I would first have to pay the landing fee. It was only two dollars, but what a difference from the treatment down south. So Southern hospitality was true, after all.

In 1974, I decided to show my device again at the AOPA show down in Florida. I left Teterboro on October 7, 1974, and flew down to Chesapeake airport in Virginia. As usual, I showed my unit everywhere that I stopped, and there was a lot of great interest in it. The next fuel stop was in Georgetown, South Carolina, a little below Myrtle Beach. I remember that the attitude there was not too friendly and a bit hostile. Maybe it was because I was a northerner? From there I continued south, but when I got to the Jacksonville area, it started getting dark, and I was in unfamiliar territory. I was just west of the city, and when I called for landing instructions, they cleared me for landing. I stayed overnight, and in the morning I had to wait for the fog to clear. When I got the clearance to take off, I went and climbed between large cumulus clouds and headed for the coastline where the sky was clear, as if you just cut off the heavy clouds with a scissor.

 I flew down along the coast, did some sightseeing at St. Augustine, and when I got near Vero Beach, I saw a line of rain clouds ahead; and although I called Vero Beach, they didn't think it was much. Since I could see the sun shining beyond the line of clouds, I just flew through a light rain and kept on going. All the airports along the coast had almost the same layout because most of them were ex-military airfields. I finally passed Palm Beach airport, and I called ahead to Fort Lauderdale airport and asked which field was theirs. They said to look for the three smokestacks. (Today you will see four smokestacks.) Well, I finally made it.

 I parked there for three days. The show was at both the field and the Diplomat Hotel. In those days, Fort Lauderdale-Hollywood Airport was more for general aviation than today. They had two runways then. Now they have three runways. Today it's called an International Airport. After the three days, I paid my parking bill, which was a whopping six dollars. (I wonder what it would be on today's market.) And I left to go home to New York.

 The trip back was a bit uneventful, but when I reached Atlantic City, I was told that Teterboro was socked in by thunderstorms. I landed at Bader Field (which is gone now) and went to a motel on Pacific Avenue. At that time there were no casinos, and I was advised to take a taxi to any eatery and not to do much walking. Anyway the next day I flew home. Good old Bader Field—that's where I invented my parking device.

I still haven't come public with my parking unit for airplanes. I've simplified it, and I do think that I will make an attempt to put it out since no one has ever come out with any device like mine. I believe it is very useful to carry it in an airplane, like you carry an emergency jack in your car. As I said before, I've flown to a lot of airports where they don't have tie-down facilities for transient pilots. Even when I used to fly to Buffalo, New York, to work for QRS, they would only put a chock in front of my wheels but no tie-down. If you should, by any chance, drive by some private airports, you will see that they are still using ropes or chains.

When I mentioned chocks before, it reminded me of another one of my inventions that I never produced. I designed an aluminum chock that was U-shaped with L-shaped legs, and then designed two straps to fit over the wheel, or the wheel pants, to lock into that U-shaped chock. By putting a locking device on that unit, you can prevent stealing the unit or the airplane. I thought of a name which you my laugh at: buy my Chockstraps! Ha-ha!

Then I invented another travel device that was also good for teaching cross-country travel. It was something I called "Line-O-Site." It was a 10 × 14 corkboard (solid cork, because a veneered corkboard will not accept pushpins in the same hole) with an aluminum frame and a clip to hold a map. I used elastic colored strings (made for me by an embroidery place) to give quick information to the pilot. I used big-sized pushpins (high necks) and used elastic strings with nooselike ends to fit easily on the heads of those pushpins.

You folded the map and put it on the corkboard and held it in place with the clip. You put black elastic strings on two pushpins. You pinned the departure airport, then stretched the string and pinned the destination airport. Now you had a course line that stood out on your map. You don't have to use a marker and mark up your map. It's like using a 3-dimensional aid. You used a green elastic string on two pushpins to show where the nearest omni stations were. You used red elastic strings on pushpins to show where the hazards were. There was a transparent compass rose that you placed along your course line—under the black string—and this would show instantly which heading to use. The compass rose was aligned with the nearest omin circle. There was a ruler to show mileage, marked off in either nautical or statute miles. There was a pad of sheets that had been marked off for planning headings, frequencies to use, and any other information that you would need for you trip.

Line-O-Site was a pretty good seller for me. You could use it in schools for teaching, you could carry it in your plane, and I was selling that unit in the United States and Canada. Today, 2010, you have the GPS units to show you the way to fly, but I read in the aviation magazines that all pilots should still learn basic pilotage skills, in case the electronic units fail. I wish I could have said the same for my Tysafe device. Still I got to sell one invention, and I'm going to try to put out Tysafe as soon as I can. It's been redesigned and simplified, and I'll try my best to find the time to make it and put it on the market.

Other little tidbits of information. I got my commercial rating on October 10, 1967. Not that I was going to go in for making money for flying. The purpose of that rating was for improving my skills. I tried to get to all airports and fly all types of aircraft. Some of the airports that I flew from were interesting, such as the Skytop airport in Roscoe, New York. It had a small eighteen hundred-foot grass runway, but it was considered a one-way runway. It was not flat but sloped up at about a thirty-degree angle. You flew down the hill to take off, and you landed uphill for the return, regardless of which way the wind was blowing. At the bottom of that runway was a cutoff drop, and you better be flying when you got there. Coming back, you didn't have to use the brakes to slow the plane down once you landed but still had to keep the power on to prevent rollback or to get to the top of the hill. I could say that it was like flying off and on an aircraft carrier. It was safe, as long as you knew what you're doing!

Now I'm going to explain about runway numbers and what they mean. Runway numbers are based on compass headings minus the last zero. For instance at LaGuardia Airport they have two runways with four headings. They have Runway 13-31 and Runway 4-22. Which way the wind is blowing will determine which runway they will use both for takeoffs and landings. The procedure is that you take off and land into the wind. Taking off into the wind gives you lift for climbing out, while landing into the wind aids in slowing down your aircraft.

Runway number 4 means you are heading 040 degrees northeast, and Runway 22 means you are heading 220 degrees southwest. The quick easy figure for pilots is the number 18. Eighteen is the reciprocating number to get a quick answer for the runways. Example 4 + 18 = 22, while 22 - 18 = 4. That is the whole trick of knowing about runway numbers. It's not difficult!

There is one more trick to learn, and that is there are parallel runways at some airports, and they use the suffix letter "R" for right and "L" for left after the runway number. For example, at the Fort Lauderdale-Hollywood Airport in Florida, they use two parallel runways; the airlines and jets use 9L and 27R (about eight thousand feet long), and the smaller general aviation planes use 9R and 27L (about five thousand feet long). They also have Runway 13-33 for emergency use. This is a foolproof system and works well.

There was the time that I took Laurie and her boyfriend Larry up for a flight; that was May 14, 1967. I rented a plane, a Cessna 172, at the marine terminal at LaGuardia Airport (you could rent planes then), and I took them up for a sightseeing flight around New York. We flew down the Hudson; and then coming back up the East River, I called the tower at LaGuardia and asked if I could land on Runway 4, which was right ahead of me. They said no and that I was number 4 to land on Runway 13. That meant I would have to follow the planes ahead of me and go north of the airport, turn left, and come around the Bronx toward the Hudson, then turn left and come across the Hell Gate Bridge over the East River, and land on Runway 13.

Behind me, over the East River, was a United 727, and I tried to keep up my speed, which was only about 124 mph. I asked the tower again if I could land Runway 4 as long as I was on a long final for that runway, and again they said negative, and I should keep up my speed and follow the other airliners ahead of me. I kept up my speed, came around the Bronx, and then over the Hell Gate Bridge. United kept asking me to "expedite, please," and I was flying with full throttle. I wanted the tower to give me a 360 turn (get out of line and make a circle to get back in), but they just asked me to expedite. I put on full flaps and dived down to the runway and landed. I got off the runway fast, and United came in right behind me and thanked me for expediting the landing. I would have preferred if the tower gave me the 360, but they didn't. It was an experience I would rather not have had.

There was the time I took Florrie for a thanksgiving dinner to the Flying W Ranch in New Jersey. I rented a plane at Morristown, and because it was a first rental, they sent a check pilot with me to insure that I knew how to fly. I didn't care and invited him to dinner. We got to the Flying W Ranch, had dinner, and then started to go home. As we did our takeoff, we ran into some low clouds, and the checkout pilot got a bit panicky and made me go back and land. You could see the moon, and when I called Morristown, they said it was very clear there too. But the check pilot insisted I stay at the Flying W Ranch till morning. So I had to RON (remain over night) and wait for the morning to go back home. That was November 28, 1963. It's nice to have logbooks.

On August 6, 1967, I rented a plane at Wurtsboro, New York, just to go fly and flew to Danbury, Connecticut. When I landed and parked next to another aircraft, I recognized the pilot as Robert Cummings, the movie actor. We had a nice chat for about an hour, and then we both went our ways.

Hi Babit

In September of 1967, Florrie spent some time at the Seton Inn Spa near Lakewood, New Jersey. I know I took a lot of photos of the fall colors there and also took Florrie flying at the old Asbury Park airport. I took aerial photos of the sunsets and had some scenic pleasure flights around the area.

In late 1967, I wanted to get a CFI rating. CFI means certified flight instructor. I felt that I could teach flying as well as teaching music. And of course, I could get paid for flying, which I loved to do. I started to take the necessary instruction for that rating. I was told that they did not give spins anymore on the flight test for CFI. Although a spin is really a safe maneuver, you have to know how to do it, and I was never taught spin maneuvers.

Let me explain about spins. I flew with Jimmy Scolaro, who was supposed to be a great instructor. We were at Little Ferry, New Jersey. And I was going to fly an Aeronca seaplane. Jimmy asked me, when we were airborne, if I ever did any spins; and when I said no, he just put the plane into a spin and made me a little sick and wobbly. That, of course, soured me on spins. A few months later, when I decided to go for aerobatic training, I rented a Citabria at Teterboro Airport. As we taxied out to the active runway, the instructor mentioned that since we have one hundred fifty horses in that engine, we should keep the stick back and the tail down; and as we got up speed, we'd take off. That bit of advice clued me into how to fly conventional gear, or tail wheel, airplanes. I was having a bit of trouble with tail wheel planes, because they always veered to the left on takeoff. I would ask why, and the answer was always that the veering to the left was called the P-factor because of the direction

The Flying Piano Roll Man

in which the propeller turned and that I needed more time in tail wheel planes. They never did explain the proper way to hold the controls for the takeoff, but I learned it that day with the Citabria.

As we flew up to the practice area for the aerobatic practice, the instructor asked me if I knew what a snap roll was. When I answered that I didn't, he did a snap roll, and then told me that it was a spin in the horizontal, as a regular spin was in the vertical. That snap roll made my stomach go in circles, and again I didn't like spins. I felt that I didn't have to worry about doing that for my coming test.

I finally got my check ride for the CFI rating; and on August 8, 1968, I took a 150 Cessna from Lamm Aviation at Teterboro for my check-ride test. The inspector's name was Claus. We flew northwest of Teterboro and did some maneuvers. Since I was going for a CFI rating, I sat right seat instead of left seat, which was always the seat for the PIC (pilot in command). When Claus asked me to take the plane up to four thousand feet, I had the feeling that he was going to ask me for a spin. Well, I was right. He asked me for a one-and-a-half turn spin to the right, and I said negative. I started making excuses, that I was rusty, and hadn't done spins in a long time. He said that I should relax and that he would take over.

To get into a spin, you have to get the nose of the airplane up, as if you're climbing; lower the engine speed; and approach a stall. Let me explain that stalling an aircraft doesn't mean you are losing your engine; it just means that you are losing forward flying speed. A good landing of an aircraft means coming in at the slowest, safest, near-stalling speed to touchdown. I mentioned about slow controlled speed before when I talked about the glassy-water landings I used for night flying. The spin is entered by cross controlling your aircraft. Ordinary turns in an aircraft are made by coordinating the rudder with the ailerons for turns. In a spin attempt, you move the controls opposite of what you do ordinarily. That's why it is called cross controlling.

Mr. Claus kept the nose of that 150 up, and I figured that he was going to do a spin. I watched as he got the nose higher, and then banked to the right and went into the spin. This time I didn't get sick because I watched his every move. When I said that I could do it, he declined and pulled another trick. He said that I just lost my engine and that I was to make a complete emergency landing.

I looked around and saw that I was over the Greenwood Lake Airport, and I spiraled down and made a complete landing from four thousand feet. He applauded me and told me to go back to Teterboro. I thought that I passed my test; but when we landed, he disapproved, telling me to go out and practice spins so that if a student made mistakes, I could take over and correct things safely. PS I never did get my CFI rating. I was too busy working and didn't take the time to go after it. But to prove that I could do spins, I flew up to Wurtsboro and rented another Citabria and took along the check pilot. I flew out over Route 17, and I tried a couple of spins, and the check pilot said that I did OK. Now I was sure that I could do spins, but, as I said, I didn't go after the CFI rating. I don't feel sorry that I didn't pursue it.

I mentioned ratings. The next rating I was going to go after was the instrument rating or IFR rating. This

The Flying Piano Roll Man

rating would allow me to fly in bad weather under the control of ATC (air traffic control). I studied for it, but I never had the time to really go after it. Of course, having an IFR rating didn't mean you were an excellent pilot. I had one experience when I was using the Lamm Air company at Teterboro and renting their planes. I had used their 152 Cessna for that instructor-test ride that I mentioned above.

I was there one evening, and I was asked about sharing a trip to the Bridgeport airport in Connecticut for one of those twenty-five-dollar hamburger flights. That's what they called those flights that were just to go for a ride. Now it's known as the one-hundred-dollar hamburger flight because of today's higher prices. I was going to share the expense of a 172 with a fellow who had just gotten his instrument rating. The other two guys were going to fly to Bridgeport in a Cessna 210, which was much faster than our 172. I was going to fly there, and the other fellow was going to fly the plane home. We took off and got to Bridgeport first. When the second plane arrived, they told us that they took longer because they were trying out an ILS system at New Haven. So we had our hamburgers, and now we were going to fly back to Teterboro.

I sat right seat, and we took off first on Runway 16, which is a south takeoff over Long Island sound. Instead of turning right after the takeoff, the pilot just flew straight ahead, toward Long Island. I asked him about making that right turn, and he replied that he knew what he was doing. So I kept quiet and watched as the shore of Long Island was coming up. I mentioned that I could see the Kennedy Airport lights to our right southwest and that we were approaching Huntington on Long Island. He finally admitted his mistake. So we turned right and flew the north edge of Long Island toward LaGuardia and reported over that field that we were just transiting the area. You can't just fly over LaGuardia today. That's trouble. When we finally got to Teterboro and landed, we were asked why it took so long, and I had to tell them that the new instrument rated pilot didn't know his way back. So sometimes a rating doesn't mean you're good.

I had another interesting twenty-five-dollar hamburger flight from Teterboro to Montgomery Airport in Upstate New York. As I was having my burger, I noticed a storm coming up fast. Since my plane was not chocked, I ran out and got into it, started the engine, and faced it into the coming thunderstorm. I kept the motor racing and using the controls to fight the wind, and when the storm passed, I shut down the engine and went back to my burger. Some pilots came to me and said, "You must be an old-time pilot to do what you just did." I laughed about it, but I used my head.

Maybe it's called just plain common sense!

I belonged to the Civil Air Patrol (CAP), and I tried to get in a lot of flying without much cost. They had a 172 and a Piper PA-18, which was also known as Super Cub, at Miller Field in Staten Island, New York, which had a grass field. One of the squadrons had a T-34, which was like a military aircraft. I was told that it really was a Beechcraft Bonanza, but instead of having four seats, it was configured in a military two-seat tandem trainer. It seems that only the big brass in the squadrons could get to fly the T-34. Being of lower rank, I had to forget about it. There is politics even in the CAP units.

The Flying Piano Roll Man

In the summer of 1968, I was playing at Ackerman's Hotel in Mount Freedom, New Jersey, and I went to the Morristown airport and found that they had a local CAP chapter there. They also had a T-34, and I learned that I could get instruction in it and fly it, so that's what I did. You had to fly that plane by the numbers. It seems that if it's military, it has to be by the numbers. I acquired a nice number of hours in that T-34. Previously I mentioned in the piano-roll chapter that I made rolls by the numbers. I said then that I also flew by the numbers. So whether I made piano rolls or flew airplanes, I did them both—by the numbers!

On one of our training flights from Morristown to Sussex, as I approached the airport, I had the T-34 trimmed for landing; and I looked up and saw that an airplane was about to land at the opposite end of the runway. I pushed the throttle in and made a right climbing turn from there, and the instructor asked me why I did that, and I pointed out the other plane about to land on the same runway but from the opposite direction. The instructor commented, that's why we practice and why it's necessary to always be alert and watching for traffic when landing at any airport.

Being with the CAP had a lot of advantages. I flew cadets for their introduction to flying. I flew on search missions, called SARCAP. Some of the flights were in the winter months; and the plane I had to fly, the Piper Super Cub, had no heater control. So we had to really be bundled up. Of course, no problem in the summertime.

On most search missions, we had to fly low to be able to see more clearly where there may be a crashed or lost plane. Sometimes we were told to fly about four hundred to five hundred feet above the ground to observe more easily. We had an observer in the rear seat, and we were given search grids to cover. Most times we would fly to an airport that was the base of operations where they would give us our search grid areas.

In a way it was exciting because most of the time we would get a call at night and have to be there in the morning to take off for where the base of operations was. Sometimes we found our quarry, and a lot of times we couldn't. For instance, we would have to look for a white plane lost in the snow. In the mountains we would have to look for something in the trees. That's why we would have to fly low. I don't think we were ever asked to fly in bad weather for searches. But getting free time flying was great.

In March of 1969, I joined the Sparton Aero Club. They had branches at a few airports. They had chapters at Teterboro, Caldwell, (both in New Jersey) and at Republic out on Long Island, New York. They had a variety of planes. They had the new Yankee, a low-winged two-seater, and a couple of Cherokees (Piper), which included the 140, the 180, and also the Arrow, which was a retractable low-wing plane. I used those planes to build up time in different models. I took passengers to air shows and to places to eat for that twenty-five-dollar hamburger. It sure was a lot of fun. There were also poker runs where you flew to some designated airports and picked up a playing card, and the winner of the poker run was the one with the best hand. No money was involved, just your presence and your own gas money. There were other contests to participate in to make flying fun and enjoyable. It reminded me of the motorcycle rallies that I used to attend where they had hill-climbing contests, or just racetracks to run around on.

While most of the times that I flew were enjoyable, there were times when you could get little frightening moments. I believe I read of a flyer's statement of "hours of joy and moments of terror." There was the time that I flew a Cherokee from Teterboro to Reading, Pennsylvania, for the big air show. When I landed and was told where to park, I noticed that they had just mowed the grass, and I saw some grass being sucked up into the engine area as I was shutting down. The whirling propeller sometimes acted like a vacuum cleaner and sucked up debris. I thought nothing of it.

When it was time to go home, I opened the cowling of the airplane to check the oil and the insides, the way we were taught to do. I saw some of that grass lying between the cylinders and figured that when I started the engine the grass would be blown out. It took about fifteen to twenty minutes before I got to the takeoff position (there were a lot of planes). When I got the clearance, I started to take off and climb out. About one hundred feet up, I smelled grass burning, and I started to make calls for a return to the landing runway. The smell only lasted for a few seconds (felt longer) and dissipated. I relaxed and continued my flight home. I was glad that I didn't have to declare an emergency and go back to land.

The next time I had a similar experience was when I owned my own airplane, and I was departing from Teterboro (where I was based) for a trip. As I climbed out and got over the Hudson River just past the George Washington Bridge, I smelled the odor of an electrical fire. I called the tower and told them but that there was no smoke or flames, and they gave me a quick reply to do a 180 (about face or U-turn) and land on Runway 24. As I came in for the landing, there were fire trucks, and when I stopped, an FAA inspector came over.

He also smelled the fumes, and then asked me if I had just annualed the plane. An annual is a yearly checkup for aircraft. When I told him that this was the first flight out after the annual, he laughed and said that the gunk they put on the engine to clean it with made it smell like an electrical fire when the engine got warm. Now I know, but it sure as hell scares you a little when you don't know the answer to certain things, and you find out the hard way! The mechanics who annual a plane should tell their customer what to expect. This way there is no surprises to encounter.

There was another close call, which didn't teach me anything for that later engine-failure incident when I owned my own plane. It was a trip to Reading for that international air show, and I rented a Cherokee 140 and took my niece Ellen, her husband, and two kids to see the show. I didn't want full tanks because it was hot and a full plane. I refused the offer of getting gas at Reading for the return flight. I monitored the gas gauges and got back to Teterboro.

The next morning I was going back to Reading. I called the gas truck and asked to fill the tanks to full since I was flying alone. While I waited for the truck, I thought I'd look inside the fuel tanks, since it was a low-winged aircraft, and I could look down into the fuel tanks. I opened the first tank and gulped. I could see the bottom. I went to the other wing and looked

The Flying Piano Roll Man

into that fuel tank, and again I gulped. I could see the bottom of that tank also. That meant I came back the night before on just fumes. I realized that I had a close call.

There was a time, about the spring of 1964, when I happened to be near Colts Neck Airport, and I wanted to fly the new Beech Musketeer. The manager whom I knew from the Red Bank airport wasn't there, so whoever was taking his place to run the airport said that he would have to check me out. It is not like renting a car where you just have to show your license. In the flying world, you have to be checked out with an instructor before you can rent a plane. They had two Musketeers on the field that had just been washed, and I was told to pick one.

I preflighted the airplane, and the check pilot and I got in and took off. As I got up to about one thousand feet, the check pilot yelled for me to go back and land immediately. I asked him what the problem was, and he pointed to the instrument panel and said that nothing was working. All the gauges were dead. I said it was no problem, that I knew what to do. I made a U-turn and came back and landed. In a high voice, he asked me where I learned to fly like that. I asked what I did wrong; and he said that I did nothing wrong but that I flew the plane without instruments; and I told him it was no problem because I could see, feel, and hear what the airplane was doing. Driving a car is the same—you see, feel, and hear what the car is doing. You don't look at the instrument panel in a car unless it's necessary. You know what sounds are normal, and when you hear something that's not normal, then you wake up and look around. The answer for the lack of instruments comes from the fact that the plane was just washed, and some water must have gotten into the static holes. Since there was no way for air to circulate, then the gauges didn't move and looked dead. I made a point of checking static holes in the future.

In 1964 I also went to Wurtsboro in Sullivan County in Upstate New York to start glider training. I felt that I should know about gliding, in case I was ever in a position where I lost an engine and had to know how to glide for distance and find a place to land. I had to make a set of takeoffs and landings before I could solo. I was in a tandem two-seater, and the instructor was in the back. Every time we took off, he would tell me to tap the altimeter window, which I would do, but I don't recall him explaining to me why I had to do it. At Wurtsboro when we would land south, our downwind leg was next to a hill with an old mine shaft as a reference point. When we were at the same height as the mine shaft, then we were at right height for our pattern run.

I have to explain what a pattern is in flying. Most patterns are left turns, and first you fly downwind with the landing runway on your left. After you pass the end of the runway, you fly about a quarter mile past and make a left turn called the base leg. When you get abreast of the runway, you make a left turn called the final leg, and you pace yourself to slow the plane and go lower and make your landing. Most airports have a standard left turn pattern, but there are a few where a right pattern is recommended.

Came the day when I was told that I could now go up solo in the glider. I was given the old instructions to come in over the field at a thousand feet and make the pattern run. Well, when I came in over the field after my first solo, I noticed that the mine shaft was higher than it should be at my indicated one thousand feet in the glider. Since I didn't have an engine to make my complete legs of downwind, base, and final, I made a decision to come in for landing at the midfield point. I came in over the trees and landed on the grass and not on the runway where I was supposed to. The owner, Tony Barone, came to me and asked why I made that type of landing instead of a complete pattern run; and I told him that the altimeter read higher than I knew I was. I knew I was too low to make a pattern run and decided to come in to land where I did. He then asked me if I kept tapping the altimeter window. I asked why would I have to do that, and he said that because the glider has no engine to keep the altimeter vibrating. Tony Barone used an old flyer's statement when I landed that glider. He said, "You almost bought the farm!" That is a statement meaning, "You almost got killed." I've only heard it among flyers, not anyplace else.

You have to tap the window so that the altimeter can adjust to the right height. I told Tony that it was never explained to me like that, and that's why I didn't keep tapping the window. It's the old story. There are a lot of times when an instructor fails to give full advice. I remember asking Tony what I was doing wrong in tail wheel flying, and as good an instructor as he was supposed to be, his answer was that you need more time and practice in tail wheel planes. He did not elaborate on how to use the controls, but as I said before, I found out the right way when I went for aerobatic training in the Citabria. As usual, I learned something the hard way.

When I got my patent on the parking device for aircraft in 1972, I started to look for an airplane and finally settled on the Cessna 172 Skyhawk no. N3500S. I bought it on May 13, 1972. It was a 1964 model E, with about one thousand two hundred hours on it. It was the last model made with the manual flaps. The following year Cessna installed electric flaps. I preferred the manual flaps because I could control it better. I was told that the electric flaps would sometimes fail, and I felt that it was safer to rely on manual control. I could, as the saying goes, milk the flaps the way I wanted to control, making the landings much smoother and slower. I always looked to develop habits for safer flying because I always said I'm a devout coward!

Another incident happened when I had my own plane. I had the habit of trimming (that's a little wheel device to help in making the controls lighter for easy flying) for a smooth takeoff at Teterboro because they had long runways. I thought that by trimming forward to lower the nose for picking up speed for takeoff and then trimming back slowly I would raise the nose and make what I would call a smooth airliner takeoff. As I said before, I was always looking for good habits, but sometimes?

I was already remarried in 1975, and a couple of years later, I took Marilyn and her daughter for a flight to Birchwood, Pennsylvania, for lunch in a hotel that had a restaurant designed like a World War I tavern, with all the insignias of the US, RAF, and German signs. It was a small airport with a two-thousand-five-hundred-foot runway and trees at both ends. We flew there, had a nice luncheon, and then got into the plane to fly home. I did my usual forward trimming and started the

The Flying Piano Roll Man

takeoff. As we were rolling along, I pointed out the scenery and looked forward and saw the trees coming closer and realized I had a short runway and had to get off quickly.

I pulled back on the yoke, but the plane wanted to stay on the ground. I finally pulled back strongly, and we took off, and I turned right and flew between two trees. I'm thinking that if anyone watched my takeoff, thinking that I'm a hotshot pilot, they wouldn't realize that I got a big fright then. Most of the procedures at airports are to take off and turn left. Maybe that airport had a right-turn procedure because I did turn right. The plane wanted to go down, and I wanted to go up, and I was hedgehopping over the trees for the next ten miles or so. I couldn't figure out what was happening, and then reached down and moved the trim wheel back. Wow! I jumped up higher in altitude, and I mentally chided myself for being so stupid. But again, I learned the hard way. I didn't tell my passengers what I had done, or showed them my feelings.

I once had to use Birchwood Airport as an emergency landing place. I was leaving Buffalo one time after I made a couple of piano rolls there, and I was on my way back to go play at Donaghy's. Flight service warned me of a storm at Teterboro Airport but that if I took my time flying back, I should miss it. It was nice and clear at Buffalo, and I took off. Getting near Elmira I started to run into some rain, but the view ahead was good. I've flown in rain and didn't think it was a big deal. When I got to the Delaware Water Gap area, I saw the ceiling get a bit lower, but I crossed the ridge of hills there and found myself in the clouds. I made a fast 180 U-turn, and I found myself flying lower over the treetops. I chided myself for getting into that predicament, mentally thinking that I read accident reports and now I had done the same stupid thing that I should have known about.

I flew over a hotel and saw the name Mount Airy. I was in the Poconos, and I looked ahead and—lo and behold—there was Birchwood Airport right in front of me. What a beautiful sight. I came in and landed. They were surprised to see someone flying in that kind of weather. I asked them to give me a lift to Stroudsburg to get a bus to get to work at Donaghy's. Looking out from the bus windows, I was happy that I didn't try to fly home to Teterboro. I saw that the clouds were down to the hilltops. I would never have made it.

I got to the restaurant a couple of minutes late. The next day was good for flying, and I went out to Teterboro and asked if anyone was going for just a flight. I latched on to one pilot and offered him ten dollars to fly me to Birchwood. He flew me there; I picked up my plane and flew it home.

There were all kinds of emergency maneuvers to learn. One was a go-around procedure with full flaps. One day I had to use it, and I felt like calling the tower and admonishing them for the way they did it. I was coming in for a landing at Teterboro, and I had full flaps on and was just about to touch down on Runway 19 when the tower yelled, "3500 Sierra, make an immediate go-around." I saw that someone had come up the taxi way to the edge of where Runway 19 and 24 met, and that plane got onto my landing runway, and then moved onto Runway 24 for his takeoff. I had plenty of room to continue my landing, but I had to follow the tower's command to go around.

I think that if a student had been flying that landing and pushed in the throttle for full power to go around, if he didn't have the practice to know what to do with a full flaps go-around maneuver, he could have stalled the plane and crashed because, with full flaps and full power, you have to lower the nose and slowly milk off the flaps to be on the safe side. With a sudden move of full power and full flaps, the airplane would climb quickly and lose airspeed and get into a stall position, which is dangerous, that close to the ground. I thought of calling the tower about it, but I just made my go-around and landed.

There were many times, if it was a nice night, that I went flying at one or two o'clock in the morning after finishing playing at Donaghy's restaurant. Sometimes I pulled some practical jokes, so to say. I took Marilyn and her friend Norma and husband up one night for a flight. On the way back to land, I jokingly asked Marilyn to look for the handbook on the method of landing. That, of course, scared my passengers in the backseat; and when I finally landed, I explained that it was just a joke. I did not do that again with future passengers.

I would like to tell a little story about smoking and flying. I used to smoke cigarettes from the teen times until I took up flying. I had the usual coughing and body aches until I read in one of my magazines that the nicotine clobbers up the filters in the airplane instruments. The airliners also banned smoking because of the effects of nicotine. I also saw pictures of what it could do to the lungs, so I stopped smoking.

In later years, the '80s, I was out in Las Vegas with Marilyn, and I decided to rent an airplane at Henderson

Airfield and do some aerial sightseeing over the Grand Canyon area. I checked out in a Cessna 182 because it had more power than my 172, and we took off. I flew over the Hoover Dam, took photos, and then continued out over the canyon. I kept climbing but was still only about one thousand feet over the ground. We saw beautiful vistas, and I finally got up to about ten thousand five hundred feet, and Marilyn said that she couldn't breathe at that altitude. We were about halfway to the Grand Canyon airport when I had to turn back.

Marilyn was a heavy smoker, and I realized that because of that, she couldn't breathe at that altitude. So we flew back to the airport, and that was it for scenic flying around Vegas. I'm not preaching, but I'm sure you smokers understand.

Before I sold my plane I was looking for excuses to go flying someplace, and since I had a few tuning clients who had moved to Upstate New York or Connecticut, I made appointments to fly out for the tuning jobs. My clients used to brag: my tuner comes with his own airplane. But I had an excuse to go flying. I finally sold my airplane in 1989 after using it for seventeen years. In the early 1980s and until 1989 when I finally sold my airplane, I noticed that I did a lot of flying to Atlantic City for the gambling. Beats driving and it was more fun.

I recently heard from my cousin Steve Rubin, who told me that he had bought a new Cessna Mustang, which is a jet plane; and since he was told that the plane is tail heavy and needed a tail-stand device to help load the plane, he inquired about my ability to make a folding tail stand to use with his plane. This, of course, gives me another incentive to start working again on my airplane-parking device. I think that I may be able to work something out for him, as well as for me.

I miss the flying, but with the new SLAs (light sport aircraft), I can start flying again, because all you need is an auto driver's license. For years I had to go through an annual medical test to be legitimate for flying. Your license is good for your lifetime, but you need a current medical to be able to rent or fly anywhere. I'm not going to go for a current medical, but I say that as long as I can drive, I can fly. So we'll see how soon I can get back to flying.

When I mentioned some pages back about looking at the instrument panel, I didn't want to imply that you don't have to look at that instrument panel. You constantly do double check between looking out and checking your instrument panel for speed control, heading awareness, stability awareness, altitude changes, etc. You just don't look out and observe the scenery. A safe pilot constantly keeps his eyes moving for traffic and airplane control. It is called scanning—outside and inside.

When you fly VFR, clear weather and not under control of the ATC (Air Traffic Control), which I did, then you are on your own to see and observe. When you fly IFR, which is under strict ATC, and the weather is bad, then you have no option but to monitor your instrument panel constantly. You RELY on it! The ATC guides you.

Flying is really safe if you use common sense and follow the rules. To me, flying is relaxing! Safe landings were done by using partial power from pattern to final and aiming for the numbers. Never missed with that system and passengers were always satisfied.

Chapter 7

My Inventions: Good, Bad, Indifferent, Questionable

In 1953, I started to keep a record of my so-called inventions. I mentioned about my model airplane aileron's position to create certain airplane abilities. It later proved to be the device we call flaps on all airplanes. Speaking of ailerons, I must say that when I bought my airplane, a Cessna 172, also called Skyhawk, I did notice that my takeoffs were rather short. It would only take about five hundred to six hundred feet to take off compared to the average of about one thousand feet.

At my first annual, I was told that my ailerons were out of rig. They were a little loose and hanging down slightly. When it was corrected, my takeoffs were a little bit longer than before. I started to think that the slight loose ailerons were acting like when you use a notch of flaps for shorter takeoffs at short runways. I realized that while at low speeds, my originally set ailerons drooped a little; and that at cruising speeds, they aligned and streamlined at the regular positions. I thought that if all airplanes were configured with loose-set ailerons, that would help for shorter takeoffs but would not change their cruising speeds. I thought of an after-market device that could be attached to the regular flaps to be slightly loose for takeoff and landing but that at cruising speeds they would be streamlined with the wing. But that was only an idea of mine, and I'm sure that the aircraft companies would not consider it valid.

In the '40s I thought of a baby-bottle holder that you could put into the baby's crib, or carriage, and that a baby, from instinct, would turn its head to reach the nipple to drink from that bottle. It was just an idea, and I didn't follow through with it. Another idea that I had for babies was a baby carriage with automatic brakes that worked from the pushing or holding handle. If you took your hands off the handle of the carriage, it would not roll. That would be very good on hilly streets as well as any surface. That idea was about forty or fifty years ago, and I still don't know why baby-carriage manufacturers have not come out with a safety device like that.

Of course, when I did my trestle set invention for model railroads, I started to work on associated model railroad ideas. I have a few listed in that little loose-leaf notebook of my inventions, with the dates of each one. Most of those listed inventions have dates starting April or May of 1953. I didn't follow through with the development of them, either because I was ⸺ the music work or I was just interrupted with gs. There were accessories, such as setups for roundhouses; different kinds of bridges, such as a straight one or revolving or rising types, that would break the connections of the tracks and stop the train. Then when the tracks were again connected, the train would proceed. There was a worker's car with two characters on it and a pumping device to propel it like the real thing and a shed to park the device alongside the tracks. These were ideas to enhance model-railroad layouts. I assume that some of those ideas were used in later layouts. I do believe that the kids' figure eight with race cars that are being sold in the toy stores today came about from my figure eight with the trains. When the train sets declined or became passé, the new era was in the little race cars.

When it came to the game inventions, I also started to work on some music-learning games. There is always a better or easier way to learn things, and I tried to think of some of them. One of the ideas did lead me to the piano-roll-arranging business, when I thought of making a toy player piano for my students. So some ideas did become fruitful. I tried a music-learning game that used two keyboards with a wall that separated them; and by electrically connecting them, two students could have a small game, such as one player plays a note and it lights up on the other side, and the other student has to play that same note on his side. If he plays the right corresponding note, it will play. It the wrong note is tried, it won't sound but just buzz. As a teacher of music, I know that the pitfalls of music learning are the fault of the publishers. I will explain why.

In the United States, they still teach music by giving each note an alphabet name and a finger number. Years ago I started a new course, and I'm sorry that I didn't follow through with it. In my course, you don't use alphabet names or finger numbers because, and teachers should realize this, the student already knows numbers and the alphabet. Believe it or not, they do not look at the notes but look at either the letter name or the finger number to play something. The language of music is the notes written on paper. That note tells you where to play, when to play, and how to play. I tell students that a note of music never changes. The note that you see on the staff of lines and spaces is only one place on whichever instrument you are playing, and that will never change.

Outside of the United States, they use one system all over the world, which is also wrong in my opinion; and that system is to use "do-re-mi," etc. A major scale starts with "Do" and is followed by "re-mi-fa-sol-oa ti-do". Any musician or singer knows that "do" is the first note of a Key. If they are going to sing in the key of F, F is "do", or in the key of B-flat, then B-flat is "do". In my course of learning, as I said, there are no alphabet names or finger numbers. You only learn to read music notes and where they belong on the piano. That goes for any instrument that you want to learn. In short, a note of music, whether you play a piano, violin, clarinet, or trumpet, is only one place on that instrument. I believe that music should be taught that way. But some teachers think that the student will play songs more quickly if they show them how to play the song by playing it for them (most students are copycats) and that the parents will think that the student is learning more quickly.

I heard that some guitar players are learning to play by the numbers. They do not read music, but they can play a song. I can show someone how to play a song, but while they can play, they don't know music. They can't read a sheet of music to learn, like they can read a book to learn. If you want to be a musician, learn to read music. It's even easier than reading a book or newspaper. There are only twelve different notes, while there are twenty-six alphabet letters to make words. I still think that it's easier to learn music. I mentioned in chapter 4 that Dr. Arthur Ellan had a mail-order music business that he made money on but that his course didn't teach anyone to read music.

I heard that a lot of the big stars on the TV circuit can compose a song, but they can't write it out. They have to give an audio tape to a knowledgeable musician to have that song put on paper. I know, because I've been asked to do those things. I take the tape, listen to it, and then write out the music using my old '98 computer.

Some of my recent crazy ideas come about usually when I'm asleep, or I laugh about it, about 6:00 a.m. in the morning. I jump out of bed and dash to my desk to write them down. I mentioned that I work for and with Danny Geoghegan who owns Danny's Pianos & Organs Store in Pompano Beach. I tune his pianos, and I've also helped with some of his inventions. He has that "magic lid" or also known as "safety-ease" device to lift the grand lid of a grand piano (which is heavy) with your pinky. He has a YouTube of his three-year-old daughter lifting and lowering a grand piano lid with one hand. I got one idea at 6:00 a.m. to automatically raise the prop stick as the grand piano lid is coming up. For some reason of business, he is delaying using that device, although he has made models utilizing that idea. But he may surprise me and use it.

Another 6:00 a.m. idea came a few months ago, and that was for a magnetic clothes hanger. I bought a magnetic toolholder, and then I went to Danny's workshop (I can use his workshop for any of my ideas) and made a working model of my magnetic clothes hanger. I tried that device with some of my heavy coats, and it works fine. You can slide the clothes side to side, and they will not fall off. The only way to get the hanger off is to break one side, and then you can release it. I looked on the Internet for any similar devices and finally found that someone in England was doing a similar thing, but not like mine. That person hung a piece of galvanized tin from the ceiling in the closet and said that you could hang the clothes any place. Well, I'm sure you don't hang clothes any place in the closet but only in one area. That person must have put a magnet on top of the clothes hanger, but I put a metal strip on the top of the clothes hanger, and all you do is reach up and put it against the magnetic strip. It's quick and easy. But I don't think that I will pursue it.

Another old idea I will mention. Years ago I wanted to make a set of "retractable" training wheels for kids' bicycles. By use of a choke cable (that's a long flexible cable with a wire inside, with a little handle at one end and bare at the other end, that you can attach to a device to activate something) to pull up the training wheels when they have enough confidence to use only the two wheels. Some of you, older player-piano people, will remember seeing choke cables used under the keyboard of a player piano to activate the muting or nickelodeon rail in the player piano.

I also thought that motorcyclists could use the same idea, but that may not make them look macho. I did see a video of someone in the British Isles with streamlined enclosed motorcycles that "had" to use retractable wheels because their legs were inside the cocoon. They could (motorcycle manufacturers) design automatic-activating retractable wheels for motorcycles so they would extend when slowing up before stopping for traffic lights or finish driving. This could be instead of a kickstand, which they use now. There's always room for improvement.

Do you remember the time—years ago—when you took an orange crate and attached a 2 × 4 wood beam and put roller skate wheels on it and ran down the street with it? Well, I designed a folding wood frame for the wheels that could fold in half into an orange crate-sized box with doors on it that you could carry to a park or ideal place then open it and unfold the leg with the skate wheels on it and run around. It could also have room for books so that you could skate to school, fold it up to go to class, and use it to skate home. It's just an idea.

You invent because of necessity. Again I used the word "necessity." I developed certain skills from necessity, and you develop inventions from necessity. I'm sure that most people can figure out something when a problem exists. You begin to use your head. Thank God, I have a craving for figuring out things, be it music or devices or whatever?

Another necessary invention, if you want to call it that, was to put wheels on my tool box, because it was getting too heavy to carry. It's only a 16 inch tool box, but I keep loading it with, what I think is, necessary tools, and it can get very heavy. I went looking for a tool box with wheels, but I couldn't find one, so I went to a store and bought a kid's back-pack with pull-out wheels for ten dollars. I went to Danny's shop and used his tools to take off the wheels unit and attach it to my tool box. I made a couple of them, because I've already broken one accidentally. At my age it becomes a handy necessary item!

I'm looking through my little loose-leaf notebook from the 1954 era and debating whether I should list the ideas I had or just skip it. A lot of those ideas I believe already came out on the market, but I didn't do them. I just had ideas, and someone else also had the same thoughts. But it's interesting to know I thought of them a lot earlier. I think you have to have the time and money to follow through with any idea. Also if any of you have any notion of taking some of my ideas and following through, be my guest. If you do, maybe you will mention that they came from me. A little stipend for my days of retirement would be appreciated, if I retire. Ha-ha!

In summation—now I sound like a lawyer—I just want to say that I developed ways and methods to accomplish ideas. In music, I play and write the way I think it should be. In songwriting, I like to tell a story and make the song more interesting. In flying, I also decided which is the safest way for me to enjoy going places. In piano-roll making I also figured ways to make it pleasurable to listen to and experimented with new ideas. So to paraphrase that certain song, "I'll do it "my way!"

People usually inquire about my health as I'm going to be ninety-three. I have my usual aches and pains. About ten or eleven years ago, I had a stent put into my arteries so my blood could move better. A few months ago, I again developed chest pains, and this time I was told that because of my age, I would be treated with only medications.

A couple of years ago, I was tuning some pianos in Palm Beach, and I got a call from my then cardiologist. I asked how he tracked me down, and he said through my sister Roz. I asked why the call, and he said, "Drop everything and go to the nearest emergency hospital." I asked why, and he said that I was losing heartbeats. I told him that I knew about that, but he explained that losing one or two heartbeats was not a big deal, but losing seven or eight heartbeats was dangerous and that I should not even drive a car. I was always told that my heartbeats were about forty-eight to fifty, and I was never told that it was dangerous. Then I found out that you have to have about sixty or more heartbeats to be normal.

This was a few days before New Year's, and I was busy playing parties and shows, and I said that I didn't have time. He asked, "Do you want to drop dead on the stage?" He had the hospital call me, and I asked if I could wait and come in Tuesday. They said OK. I went in Tuesday, and they put a pacemaker in my chest. I get checked for it every three or four months, and I laughingly say, "I have better rhythm now!"

I'm doing fine now and living an independent life. I'm busy with my piano tuning, playing parties, rehearsing shows, and doing what I want to do and when I want to do it. I come and go as I please. My sister Roz feels the same way as I do, and since she lives in the same condo as I do, we get together quite often. I will either go to her place for lunch or dinner, or we eat out, so, as the saying goes in music, we play it by ear. So here's to a happy and fruitful life.

Feel free to reach me at either of my two e-mails: *hibabit@juno.com* or *babichh@bellsouth.net*.

From AMICA Honorary Hi Babit

DEAR MR. SANTA CLAUS

HI BABIT 1973

CHRIST-MAS WILL SOON BE HERE IT'S TIME FOR SAN-TA AND HIS REIN-DEERS I

HOPE HE BRINGS THE THINGS I LIKE BUT MAYBE I BETTER SIT DOWN AND WRITE TO

DEAR MIS--TER SAN-TA CLAUS I'D LIKE TO OR-DER A HOB-BY HORSE A

HORSE THAT NEIGHS A HORSE THAT SWAYS A HORSE WHOSE TAIL WAGS DIF-RENT WAYS

DEAR MIS-TER SAN-TA CLAUS I'D LIKE A SOL-DIER FOR THAT HORSE A

IT MAKES NO NEVER MIND

CHORUS: It makes no nev-er mind, is what she said to me.
It makes no nev-er mind, means 'I don't care' you see.
It makes no nev-er mind, can al-so seem to be,
Do what you want, do what you want, do what you want with me.

1st Verse: I had a date one day last week with this here gal you see.
I was-n't late for that there date 'cause she's pret-ty as can be.
Down lov-ers lane we took a walk, and af-ter some small talk,
I asked her for a lit-tle kiss, she ans-wered me with this.

CHORUS

2nd Verse: I wined and dined this pret-ty gal, I bought her gifts and things.
I gave her pins and bra-ce-lets and then a dia-mond ring.
In lov-ers lane we parked one night, I asked her 'let's make love'.
She looked at me and the dia-mond ring and winked at the moon a-bove.

CHORUS:

3rd Verse: Our wed-ding date has now been set, we'll soon be man and wife.
For mak-ing love to her that night, she's sen-ten-ced me to life.
And then some day we may be blessed with a lit-tle mis-ter or miss.
I'll do my best, for a hap-py nest, by tell-ing my gal this.

LAST CHORUS:

It makes no nev-er mind, is what I'll say to her.
When there are things ~~we have~~ Do Them Just to do, I'll just do them ~~with~~ her.
Our hap-py lit-tle home, will al-ways be care-free.
With - it makes no nev-er mind, and - do what you want with me.

Hi BaBit
152 Clarkson Ave.
Brooklyn, New York, 11226.

I LOVE YOU I WANT YOU

HI BABIT

BUT FIRST LET'S DO THE CHA-CHA-CHA HI BABIT 1955

I WANT TO HOLD YOU EN - FOLD YOU AND MAKE LOVE TO YOU I WANT TO PLEASE YOU AND TEASE YOU AND STILL SQUEEZE YOU TOO I WANT TO KISS YOU CA - RESS YOU EM = BRACE YOU BUT FIRST LET'S DO THE CHA - CHA - CHA. CHA - CHA- CHA. I WANT YOUR ARMS ALL A - ROUND ME TO HOLD ME SO TIGHT, I WANT YOUR LIPS TO BE PRESS - ING UP - ON MINE JUST RIGHT, I WANT YOUR LOVE TO DE - LIGHT ME, EX - CITE ME BUT FIRST LET'S DO THE CHA - CHA - CHA. CHA - CHA --

IN LOVE WITH A DREAM

HI BABIT - 1975

ONCE I WOULD SAY I WAS HAP-PY ALL DAY 'CAUSE I WAS IN

LOVE I'M IN LOVE I WAS IN LOVE WITH A

DREAM I USED TO SING EACH DAY WOULD

BRING THAT WON-DER-FUL THING IT WAS LOVE I WAS IN

LOVE WITH A DREAM.

ONCE SHE WAS RE- -EL ONCE I COULD FE--- ---EL

IN LOVE WITH A DREAM

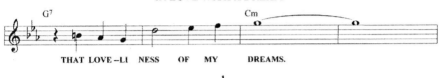
THAT LOVE—LI NESS OF MY DREAMS.

ONCE I COULD TOUCH HER KISS HER AND LOVE HER

THEN FA-DED FROM SIGHT, LIKE A DREAM. THE MEM-OR-IES

STAY, DAY AF-TER DAY STILL I MUST SAY THAT I'M IN LOVE I'M STILL IN

LOVE WITH A DREAM.
HI BABIT - 1975   954-984-0033 / 954 856-6858

CHAPLINESQUE

CHAPLINESQUE

PERPETUAL MOTION

HI BABIT

The Flying Piano Roll Man